Thy Kingdom Come

Leader's Guide

Mark Hart

Ascension Press
West Chester, Pennsylvania

Ascension Press
Post Office Box 1990
West Chester, PA 19380
Orders: 1-800-376-0520
www.AscensionPress.com
www.GreatAdventureOnline.com

Cover design: Devin Schadt

Printed in the United States of America

ISBN 978-1-934217-27-6

Contents

Introduction

Words carry a great deal of meaning. It is not a ring that begins a marital relationship—it is words. It is not a gun or a missile that usually starts a war—it is words. Words have the power to build and to destroy, to heal and to wound. Words carry meaning far beyond letters and punctuation.

The Bible is filled with words, yes, but the Bible is also the Living Word (Hebrews 4:12-13). Jesus Christ is the Word (John 1:1-4), as we are reminded by St. John. For most of us, though, the Sacred Scriptures are more "words *about* God" than "the Word of God."

If you experienced *T3: The Teen Timeline*, you hopefully came to a new understanding of the "big picture" of the Bible and your place within the story. Again, it's vital to remember that the Bible doesn't just speak *to* you; it speaks *about* you.

In this new *T3* Study, *Thy Kingdom Come*, we are going to take a much deeper, much more intimate look at the "star" of the Story, our Lord and Savior Jesus Christ.

Through the gospels, the Holy Spirit teaches us many things, but possibly nothing more important than the following simple truth:

There is no more important relationship you will ever (or could ever) have than your relationship with the Holy Trinity, through our Lord Jesus Christ.

Do you agree with the above statement? If not, why don't you? If so, does your life reflect your agreement with it?

Your entire identity as a Catholic—indeed, as a human being—is a direct reflection of the intimacy (or lack of intimacy) in your relationship with Jesus. How well do you know Jesus? What parts of your life do you let Him into and what parts do you try to keep Him out of? What areas do you try to keep as your own, in darkness, preventing the light of God to penetrate? The answers to these questions will direct your life here on earth and your eternal life.

The whole point of *Thy Kingdom Come*—and, of the Gospel as a whole—is to introduce you to the very heart of God, in Christ Jesus. The gospels are intended to teach you not only "what Jesus did and said" but who Jesus *is*—and who He calls you to become.

Through the course of this Bible Study series, you will no doubt learn a lot of facts about Jesus and the purpose of the Incarnation. You will hear a great deal about different places and characters and events. At the same time, you will hear about a God who is so in love with you that He stops at nothing to get you to heaven. This really is the entire point of the Bible and of the Church: your salvation—to get you home to heaven.

Whether or not you know a lot about Jesus, you're about to encounter Him and hear a ton of information about Him.

Some of you know Jesus as a teacher; others think of Him as a healer. Some going through *Thy Kingdom Come* might think of Him more as a narrative character. While all of these views are true, we must never forget that Jesus Christ is our Savior and our Lord.

As you begin *Thy Kingdom Come*, and take a step into greater understanding of Christ and intimacy with Him, pause and reflect on these words from Pope John Paul II:

> It is Jesus that you seek when you dream of happiness; he is waiting for you when nothing else you find satisfies you; he is the beauty to which you are so attracted; it is he who provokes you with that thirst for fullness that will not let you settle for compromise; it is he who urges you to shed the masks of a false life; it is he who reads in your hearts your most genuine choices, the choices that others try to stifle.
>
> It is Jesus who stirs in you the desire to do something great with your lives, the will to follow an ideal, the refusal to allow yourselves to be grounded down by mediocrity, the courage to commit yourselves humbly and patiently to improving yourselves and society.

Seek Jesus—today and throughout this study—and watch what happens.

I pray that this study blesses you, and that you will allow the power of the Gospel to radically change and transform your life, as it did (and continues to) mine.

—Mark Hart

NOTES

How Thy Kingdom Come works in conjunction with T3: The Teen Timeline

You may have already taken your teens and young adults through the initial study in the *T3* series, *T3: The Teen Timeline.* Welcome to our study of the gospel of Matthew, *Thy Kingdom Come.* If you have not yet gone through *The Teen Timeline*, don't worry, you won't be lost!

Whereas *T3: The Teen Timeline* presents teens with the "big picture" of salvation history and serves as an introduction to the Bible, *Thy Kingdom Come* seeks to accomplish three key goals:

1. <u>Present the "authentic" Jesus to your teens.</u>
   This may shatter some of the images they have of Him, images rooted more in imagination or in modern media accounts rather than in the Bible. If this is the case, praised be to God! Young people deserve to know the true Jesus, not merely their own (or others') view of Him.

2. <u>Help teens see more clearly the timeless relevance of Christ's teachings.</u>
   The Sacred Scriptures often fail to "come to life" in the minds and lives of our young people because the doctrine found in them doesn't seem practical. In short, they have little reverence because they see little relevance.

3. <u>Give teens an encounter with God's unconditional love and mercy.</u>
   While most of the young people who experience *Thy Kingdom Come* have heard that God loves them, this truth is often "known" but not "believed." Through the Scriptures shared, the stories told, and the truths taught in your live sessions and on the DVD, there will be ample opportunities for your young people to experience the love of God in a new way.

Those who went through *T3: The Teen Timeline* will be accustomed to the pacing of the DVD segments and how they interact with the Study Guides. In the coming pages, you will read more about how the DVDs work and what facets of the session overviews differ from those of *The Teen Timeline* study. Feel free to adapt the sessions to fit your specific needs, taking into account your particular timetable, group size, age range, and objectives for the study.

You will notice that a slightly different style is used in *Thy Kingdom Come.* Not having to cover as much history or as many figures as *The Teen Timeline*, this study allows the presentations (both DVD and "live") to "go deeper" into the Christological faith and moral development of your teens. The stories are more issue driven than character driven, and the challenges are more directed to the individual rather than to the group. Essentially, *Thy Kingdom Come* is an invitation for every student to spend some one-on-one contemplative time with Jesus and to grow more confident in His great mercy and unconditional love.

Before you lead, spend some time in prayer. Pray deeply. Pray often. Pray constantly (see 1 Thessalonians 5:17). Pray and trust that the Lord not only hears your prayers (see Jerermiah 29:12), but is willing to perfect your heart through them if you let Him. The more transparent and sanctified our lives become as leaders, the more our young people will be inspired to resemble the image and likeness of God in which they were created.

NOTES

How to use Thy Kingdom Come in different settings

Youth group Scripture Study

Mark Hart has successfully executed *T3* studies with hundreds of teens and young adults in parish youth group, diocesan, and retreat settings over the past few years. Depending upon the parish's specific meeting schedule and catechetical model, *T3* studies are designed to be implemented in a variety of ways.

Most youth groups move through the eight sessions over a two-month period, meeting once a week. Other groups gather on a Saturday morning with Mass and move through the eight sessions in one day (including breaks and, of course, food–after all, they are teens!). Still others meet for one night on four consecutive weeks, doing two session per week. You get the idea.

In this *Thy Kingdom Come* Leader's Guide, there are ten optional "follow-up" Bible studies. These act as a wonderful weekly "follow up" once your teenagers have gone through the *Thy Kingdom Come* material.

Ideally, this Bible study resource is designed for youth ministers, DREs, and catechists who want to present the Bible to their teens but have little time to develop programs from scratch.

Regardless of the schedule you utilize, it is important to take a few moments at the beginning of each session to:

- Review where you left off and what happened last time. The Student Workbook is a great aide in this regard.
- Encourage the teens to read through on their own the chapters covered in the session they have just gone through.
- As the teens read on their own, remind them to write down any questions they have and to bring them to your next meeting.

Classroom

Teachers often search for a way to bring the Bible to their students and keep it alive for them in their hearts. *Thy Kingdom Come* is so suited for the classroom that any teacher can use it. Each DVD segment could also serve as a resource for any session that a teacher may not be present for. Feel free to use the DVD in the classroom or in your own preparation of your *Thy Kingdom Come* session plans. The Discussion Points could be utilized as homework or classroom conversation. The important thing is to let *Thy Kingdom Come* be a starting point for deeper conversations during your class times.

Home Bible Study

Thy Kingdom Come is designed as a family-friendly resource. Utilizing communication principles, relevant timely information regarding teen culture, storytelling, and humor, this study is not just informative for teens but for parents, as well. The DVDs not only keep parents' attention, but also offer them useful, practical insights into how to present the Bible–and the entire Catholic faith, for that matter–in a way that today's teens will understand and enjoy.

Parents are encouraged to either watch the DVDs before their teens view them or, better yet, watch them with their teens over a few nights, stopping along the way to ask the teens what points most jumped out at them, confused them, or changed their perspective of God.

Confirmation

While the age of reception of the sacrament of confirmation differs depending on a given diocese, several groups have looked to *T3* Bible studies to cover a significant portion of the Scripture component of their confirmation preparation curriculum. Ideal for a "day of prayer" at the parish, a *T3* study both fulfills the catechetical necessities of teens' sacramental preparation and presents several evangelistic points that they might not be accustomed to hearing if they are not active in a parish youth group.

Prayer Meetings

Due to the informal nature of a prayer meeting and its voluntary nature, it might be best to bill *Thy Kingdom Come* as an ongoing Gospel series. Use it as a semester theme. A simple format can be: an introductory prayer (anything from praise music to a Rosary would be appropriate), followed by a quick review of what you have covered, and then into *Thy Kingdom Come.* Keep the DVD clips short so that you hold the attention of those who attend, but plan out the semester in advance so that you are not ending in the middle of a session. Use the discussion points as your own commentary or as a thought you can send the group off with. Pick a verse or even an entire segment for the group to meditate on for the prayer meeting. You might even want to gear the music and environment to the particular segment you are covering at the meeting.

Leader's Tips

As we have noted, *Thy Kingdom Come* has been designed to be utilized in a variety of settings. Bearing this in mind, there are several instructions and reminders we would like to give you in this section to insure that you gain the maximum benefit and "mileage" out of this resource.

In this section, we will cover:

- The DVD set
- The Student Workbook
- How to teach *Thy Kingdom Come* with you as the main presenter
- Tips when introducing teens to the Bible
- Additional notes regarding this *T3* resource

Using the DVD set

The four DVDs are broken into eight segments, each approximately thirty-five to forty minutes in length. Definitely view them in their entirety before showing them to the group, so that you might understand the overall content, approach, and components.

Each DVD contains two sessions:

Disc One

Session 1 – An Introduction to Thy Kingdom Come and the Gospel of St. Matthew
Session 2 – Matthew 1-3

Disc Two

Session 3 – Matthew 4-7
Session 4 – Matthew 8-15

Disc Three

Session 5 – Matthew 16 and 17
Session 6 – Matthew 18-25

Disc Four

Session 7 – Matthew 26 and 27
Session 8 – Matthew 28

It is important to note (especially for those who are familiar with any of *The Great Adventure* studies) that, while based on *The Great Adventure*, the *T3* studies take a slightly different approach given their teen/young adult demographic.

You will notice that several points, people, and stories found in the 24-week adult studies have been quickly glossed over or even omitted entirely. You will find, too, that certain other stories and teaching points are covered in exhaustive detail in *Thy Kingdom Come.* This is not to imply that the omitted points are unimportant or that those covered in greater detail here are more important. Decisions on content were made during the writing, creation, and editing of this resource to ensure that the teen demographic was given the most fundamental points in broad stroke form, while insuring that *T3* studies maintain a faster-paced, engaging and "culturally-aware" approach that keeps teenager's attention throughout.

Using the Leader's Guide

This Leader's Guide contains all of the content found in the *Thy Kingdom Come* Student Workbook, along with leader's notes and ten optional Bible studies. Some of the leader's notes are expansive, while others are quite simple; all are very practical. Read through the leader's notes prior to presenting a specific page or section.

Sections included in the workbook will be an invaluable reference in ongoing study, college, and ministry. Note, however, that the Student Workbook does not include the ten additional Bible studies, so they will not have the benefit of those studies unless you choose to utilize them from the Leader's Guide. The more you help your teens navigate through their Workbooks, the more they will get out of *Thy Kingdom Come* for years to come.

When teaching it yourself, using DVDs for reference

You might choose to use the DVDs as reference or as an outline and present the *Thy Kingdom Come* "live." If you choose this option, we encourage you to watch the series at least twice prior to beginning of the study so that you are familiar and comfortable with the material. During both the preparation and live execution of a *Thy Kingdom Come*, ask yourself the following questions:

- Do the points I am making relate to a teenager's faith walk rather than mine?
- Am I tying make biblical principles and story details relevant to a teen's life?
- Am I giving them enough of a historical perspective?
- Am I using too many personal examples that might detract from the Study?
- Am I trying to do too much? (Remember, less is often more with beginners)
- Am I prepared spiritually to lead this? (Knowledge is not enough; you must be "prayed up")
- Are my teens really ready for the entire Study, or does the "soil need to be tilled" a little more?
- Am I utilizing the resources to the best of my abilities (e.g., the DVDs, the Leader's Guide notes, the optional Bible studies and Scripture discussions, etc.)?
- Am I creating an environment that is inviting to teens? Does it feel like a class or more like an experience, a journey?
- Do the teens feel free to ask questions and am I prepared to answer them if they do?
- Is the Holy Spirit guiding this or am I?

Leader's Guidelines for Each Session

At the beginning of each session, before you pray, discuss the following with your teens:

- Tell them what session (i.e., 1 - 8) you will be studying
- Tell them what chapters of Matthew's gospel will be covered in this session

Opening Prayer

When the room is silent and the teens are ready to pray, offer the opening prayer, either the one provided or a spontaneous prayer. The prayers provided loosely follow the themes discussed in a particular session, so you may want to read through it prior to offering it.

Opening Question

The opening question should be written on a board for reflection or posed to the group, but it should not be "debated" or discussed. Have the teens write it out, just as you say it, under the "Opening Question" title bar on the corresponding session page in their Student Workbooks. There is a benefit to them writing out the question in their own handwriting.

Verse to Remember

For each session, there will be one Scripture verse picked that the teens should look up in their Bibles and transcribe (again, in their own handwriting) on the corresponding session page of their Student Workbook. This repeated exercise will not only frame the session around the verse but help also them begin to navigate the Bible more easily.

Play the DVD Session

The DVD Session overviews follow the eight sessions. Sessions 1 and 2 are on disc one, Sessions 3 and 4 are on disc two and so forth (see Leader's Tips for a full listing of discs and sessions).

Breaking it Down

The ten questions selected for each session are by no means the most important or the only facts the teens need to learn or remember. These questions are designed to ensure that the teens will be paying attention during the DVD, and to highlight specific points of interest, foundational story elements, fundamentals of the faith or basics of Christian doctrine.

During each DVD Session, the ideal learning situation would be to have the teens fill in the answers to these ten "Breaking it Down" questions (which are found in the Student Workbook) following the prompts on the DVD. Taking their own notes in the Notes spaces provided in their guides.

Encourage them ahead of time to record Scripture verses, "notepad" explanations, and other graphics that appear on the screen to further drive home important events and catechetical points.

Talking it Out

The discussion questions listed in this section refer back to the storylines and subplots that are discussed in the DVD. They can be offered in a small or large group format, depending upon group size and structure. They can even be given as questions to be written out and answered in essay form, if desired. For optimal success with the discussion questions, be willing to stay on any question that elicits a strong reaction. Don't feel that you have to get to all of them.

Thinking it Through

The questions put forth in this section serve to help the teens connect the dots between "the Gospel story" and their personal stories. The point is to help the teens see how to implement the realities and truths espoused in the Session in their daily faith walks, relationships, homes, schools and parishes.

Unlike *T3: The Teen Timeline*, the *Thy Kingdom Come* study does not include quizzes. The goal of *Thy Kingdom Come* is for teens to have a transformational encounter with Christ through the living Word of the Gospel. These encounter moments are more important than memorizing facts. As a result, rather than offering quizzes, we suggest you spend more time in activities that will encourage more contemplative prayer and discussion. Doing so will send a message to the young people that knowing the person of Jesus Christ is far more than knowing "facts" about His life.

The questions in "Thinking It Through" can be answered as essays (for teachers looking for a quantifiable "testing" component). Ideally, though, these questions function more as catalysts for journaling, allowing your teenagers to take the themes that have been presented, internalize them, and "go deeper" in their own faith journeys. Depending upon the size and maturity level of your group, you might even find that it is most effective to have a large group discussion of the "Thinking It Through" questions.

Session 1
The Royal Family

Opening Prayer

Lord God, you promised to be with us always, and You give us the gift of your living Word and the gift of your Eucharist to remind us of that everlasting promise. Open our minds today, Lord, that we would see Your face and hear Your voice in a new way. Holy Spirit, move through us as you moved through St. Matthew, and reveal to us all the ways we need to surrender to God, all the ways we can abandon our own plans and follow Christ as St. Matthew did in his lifetime. May all we do this day and in this study lead us closer to Jesus Christ and help us in our efforts to build His Church on earth. And may our Mother, the Blessed Virgin Mary join Her prayers to ours throughout this study. Amen. (*Pray a Hail Mary.)*

Before you can take a road trip, there are several things you should do, i.e., put gas in the car, stock up on food and drinks, change the oil, get ahold of a map, visit the rest room (that one last time) and, if necessary, find a safer driver than you.

Similarly, before you can really take a trip through the Bible, especially a gospel, you need to prepare yourself. You need to be alert, open (mentally and spiritually), and ready. You need to know your way around "the car," and you need a map to get you where you are going.

In this first session, try to picture yourself starting from scratch. Whether you know a ton about the gospels or very little, imagine yourself as a blank piece of paper that God desires to fill with knowledge. Then, each week, as you move deeper into the living Word of God and deeper into the heart your Savior, Jesus Christ, imagine yourself coming back again and again as a blank sheet, wanting to be filled.

The Chapters Covered in this Lesson

An Introduction to Matthew

Opening Question

Why is it important for *you* to know the Gospel?

Verse to Remember

Matthew 7:7 - "Ask and it will be given you; seek, and you will find; knock, and it will be opened to you."

Breaking it Down

1. What does the word "gospel" mean?
   Good News (*evangelium* is "good news" in Latin)

2. What was Matthew's "other name"?
   Levi (see Luke 5:27)

3. What was Matthew's profession prior to following Jesus?
   Tax collector (see 10:3)

4. What did Matthew do for Jesus after his encounter with the Lord?
   Matthew throws a great banquet feast for Jesus (see Luke 5:29).

5. To whom was St. Matthew writing his gospel?
   Matthew was writing to the Jewish people.

6. What does Matthew assume about his readers?
   Matthew assumes that his audience knows Jewish history, Jewish culture, and the Torah.

7. What are the three titles given (in Matthew 1:1) to Jesus?
   The Christ, Son of David, Son of Abraham

8. What is the term for "reading out" of the gospels, their intended meaning(s)?
   Exegesis

9. Why do the gospels "disagree" on details at times?
   There are several writers who have different perspectives of the same events.

10. What "themes" does Matthew focus on in his gospel?
   Jesus the (Messiah and) King establishing His Kingdom on earth.

Play the DVD - Disc 1, Segment 1

TALKING IT OUT

Discussion Questions

1. Why is "the journey between the head and the heart" so difficult? Why do so many people get stuck in academic questions about the existence of God or the truths about Jesus Christ? Where does faith come in?
2. Why is a relationship with Jesus Christ the most important relationship you will ever have?
3. Why would God give us Sacred Scripture and Sacred Tradition? Why not just one or the other? Why are both so vital to the truth and to the Church?

THINKING IT THROUGH

Where would you rate yourself (1 to 10) based on the question "How well do you know Jesus"? What do you need to eliminate in your life before you would rate yourself higher? What do you need to "add" into your life in order to rate yourself higher?

Session 2
Arrows Pointing to the King

Opening Prayer

God our Father, we thank you for our families. Thank you, Father, for those family members we are close to and for those we may feel far from. Lord please bless them, whether they are near or far from You. Use us, Lord, as arrows that point our families and friends back to You. Give us the humility to live simple lives of love and give us the courage to speak Your truth, even though we are imperfect in our love. May our time in this study, today, Lord build your Kingdom on earth. Mother Mary and St. Joseph please pray with us. Amen. *(Pray a Hail Mary.)*

How much of your childhood do you remember? What are the first and earliest memories you have of your childhood? How many relatives do you know? How far back (or "up") in your family tree do you know people? Do you know your great-grandparents or great-great-grandparents? What is your background, what nationalities and ethnicities make up your family tree? How important would you say these influences were (and are) in making you the person who you are today?

Your past does not dictate your present or future, but it can affect both. Knowing "where you come from" can help you get to where you want to go and, if necessary, avoid where you should not venture.

In this, the early life of Jesus, you will be given a lot of names and details that you might not find very important upon first glance. Look again. As you move through this lesson, lean in don't pull back. The harder you look, the more truths you'll discover–not only about Jesus, but about your life as well. God wants to teach you something on every page of Scripture ... so let Him.

The Chapters Covered in this Lesson

Matthew 1 - 3

Opening Question

What else would God have to do to prove to you that Jesus is God?

Verse to Remember

Matthew 2:2 - "Where is he who has been born king of the Jews? For we have seen his star in the East, and have come to worship him."

Breaking it Down

1. What are the Jews (in Palestine at this time) waiting for?
   The Messiah

2. Why is the geneology of Jesus so important for us to know?
   It is your family tree.

3. Who are the five women listed in the geneology?
Tamar, Rahab, Ruth, Bathsheba (wife of Uriah), Mary

4. Why are the women listed so important?
They all are Gentile women, but the Kingdom is for everyone. Jesus has imperfect people in his family who aren't Jewish.

5. What does the name "Emmanuel" mean?
Literally, "God is with us."

6. What were the names of the Magi, according to tradition?
Balthazar, Gaspar, Melchior

7. What do the gifts symbolize?
Gold for the royalty of Jesus, frankincense for His divinity, and myrrh for His humanity.

8. What is Matthew pointing out in Matthew 2:15?
Jesus is the new Israel and the new Moses. Jesus will lead us out of the slavery of our sin like Moses led his people out of Egypt.

9. Who was Herod and why was he dangerous?
Herod was the bloodthirsty Jewish king who tried to kill the Messiah by ordering that every male child be slaughtered at birth.

10. Why is John the Baptist so important?
John was Jesus' cousin; he is the "forerunner" prophet pointing to Jesus the Messiah.

Play the DVD - Disc 1, Segment 2

Talking it Out

Discussion Questions

1. Which is harder for you to believe, that God would make a star to announce His Son's birth or that God would humble and empty Himself, take on flesh and come into this world as a child? Explain.
2. For many people, it is safer and easier to say that "Jesus died for mankind" than it is to proclaim, "Jesus died for *me.*" Do you believe that Jesus died for you? Do you believe that you need a Savior? Why or why not? Why is this such a difficult belief?
3. When people encounter Christ they either worship Him (like the Magi) or they seek to destroy Him (like Herod). Is this a true statement? Is there a third option? Why or why not? Explain your answer using practical modern examples.

Thinking it Through

As we see in the reality of the Gospel narrative, the events surrounding Jesus' birth are anything but "perfect" (i.e. sinners in His family tree, an unexpected trip in Mary's third trimester of pregnancy, having a manger for a crib, a bloodthirsty king, a massacre of children, etc). How do these truths make you feel as a believer, thankful or skeptical? Does it make it easier or difficult for you to believe in Christ and follow Him knowing the realities surrounding His birth?

Session 3
The King Comes of Age

Opening Prayer

Lord Jesus Christ, You are like us in all things but sin. Forgive us, Lord, for all those times that we choose the worldly glamour of sin over your heavenly promise of your love. Help us to live in your image. Holy Spirit, grant us the patience and fortitude we need to grow in holiness and to avoid sin and reveal to us all those areas of our lives that we need to change, to avoid the occasions of sin we so often run toward. Father in heaven, grant us the strength to live for You. Amen. *(Pray an Our Father.)*

It is not easy living the Christian life, is it? Nothing worth having, though, is easy. The book of Hebrews tells us that Jesus was like us in all things except sin (Hebrews 4:15). It also says that we should have confidence when we go to Jesus precisely because He suffered temptation, too. Before His throne we will find grace and mercy (4:16). We needn't be afraid of Jesus; He knows us better than we know ourselves. He knows the true movements of our hearts.

It's a popular modern misconception that being a Christian—and especially a Catholic—is about "being a good person who follows rules." But that is not what the Catholic faith is about; it's much deeper than that. Living out your Catholic faith is not about being a "good" person; it's about becoming a "new" person (Galatians 2:20). In this lesson from St. Matthew's gospel we are going to see more of the human (and the practical) side of the King of Kings.

This session is a great wake-up call, especially if you've been a little lazy in your spiritual life. Don't fall into the trap of looking to the people on your right or your left and thinking "I'm not as bad as them" or "I'm far worse than them." Jesus is talking to you now. Listen carefully to what He has to say.

The Chapters Covered in this Lesson

Matthew 4 - 7

Opening Question

Does obedience make you weak or strong?

Verse to Remember

Matthew 6:21 - "For where your treasure is, there will your heart be also."

Breaking it down

1. Why does Jesus head out to the desert?
   He is led out by the Holy Spirit to be tempted by the devil.

2. Is the devil trying to get Jesus to do?
   He is trying to get Jesus to reveal His identity.

3. What weapon does the devil try to use against Jesus?
The Word of God, i.e., Sacred Scripture (Ephesians 6:17).

4. What did Jesus preach (verses 4:23-24)?
The good news of the kingdom, the healing of diseases and infirmities.

5. What does it mean to be "blessed"?
To be "highly favored" by God.

6. What does Jesus expect from us in the "New Covenant"?
He is calling you to go the extra mile, to something more.
To start judging your holiness by the God who created you.

7. What does the Our Father teach us?
To focus first on God's glory.

8. What is "mammon"?
Earthly treasures.

9. What practical advice are we given in chapter 6?
Don't be anxious.

10. What are "the two ways" that Jesus discusses?
The narrow way through Jesus which is difficult and the wide way, the way of the world, which is easier.

Play the DVD - Disc 2, Segment 1

Talking it Out

Discussion Questions

1. What do people treasure most in this world? Rate the top three worldly "treasures."
2. Based upon the amount of time you spend thinking about or doing different things, what do you treasure most, *really*?
3. What is the most practical advice, in your opinion, that Jesus offers us in the gospel? Which of Jesus' teachings do you find most relevant or makes the most sense to you, on a daily basis?

Thinking it Through

The devil knows where we are weakest. The devil attacks where we are weakest. In what areas of your life are you most prone to the attacks of the devil? What weapons do you utilize to fend off the attacks of the evil one? What weapons are available to you that you (possibly) do not take enough advantage of?

OR

Go through "The Our Father: An Overview" exercise (on page 55 of the Leader's Guide).

Session 4
Just an Average Day in the Kingdom

Opening Prayer

Lord Jesus, we believe. Help us in our unbelief. In all of those areas of our lives, Lord, in which we feel helpless and powerless ... in all of those areas, Lord, where we feel alone or unworthy ... in all of those areas, dear Jesus, in which we have lost hope, even lost hope in You ... give us strength. Call us back to You, Lord. Hear our prayer. Come to our aide in our weakness. We believe you still work miracles, Lord Jesus, help us to believe strongly enough in your love for us, that we would believe more deeply in Your active presence in our lives. Help us this day Lord to build Your kingdom on earth. Amen. *(Pray an Our Father.)*

What does your average day consist of? You probably wake up (slowly), shower (necessarily), eat breakfast (possibly), go to school or to work (begrudgingly), laugh with friends (frequently), pray (hopefully), dwell on the past (unnecessarily) or think about the future (possibly). Ever fall into that rut?

But what if your world was turned upside down by spending time with Jesus, face-to-face, each day?

Can you imagine walking with Jesus on a daily basis? Just imagine walking with Jesus as He's feeding thousands, healing lepers, raising the dead, and going toe-to-toe with smug Pharisees. That would be anything but ordinary.

Some make the mistake of viewing the Gospel stories as mere stories. Don't make that mistake. The Gospel is truth. The accounts are truth. The question is not about their validity but about your veracity. The truth is that you can encounter Jesus face-to-face every day in His sacraments, especially in the Eucharist. In this session, really push yourself to enter into the story. Picture the situations and locations. Imagine the sights and the smells. Listen carefully to the words because Jesus isn't just interacting with characters, He's interacting with you.

The Chapters Covered in this Lesson

Matthew 8 - 15

Opening Question

Do I believe that Jesus is capable and willing to work a miracle in my life?

Verse to Remember

Matthew 8:8 - "Lord I am not worthy to have you come under my roof; but only say the word, and my servant will be healed."

Breaking it Down

1. What do Christ's miracles teach us?
   Jesus has the power of God and is trying to bridge the gap between us and God.

2. What does Jesus' miracle with the demoniacs teach us?
   The demons recognize Jesus and His authority.

3. What does "the call of Matthew" teach us?
God judges us from the inside out.

4. What is the purpose of fasting?
Voluntary self-denial, your spirit leads your body.

5. What is the difference between a disciple and an apostle?
A disciple is a "follower" or student of Jesus. An apostle is "one who is sent out" with a special authority to teach the Gospel; selected from among Jesus' disciples.

6. Why did Jesus select twelve apostles?
Because there were twelve tribes of Israel. Since Jesus is the "new Israel," He is building a new structure.

7. Why does Jesus claim His "yoke" is easy?
Because God's way—i.e., following the Gospel—isn't difficult; it is what we were created for.

8. What does Jesus teach us about clean and unclean?
It is not what is outside the body that defiles us (i.e., makes it "unclean"), it is what is on the inside, in the heart.

9. What does the word "parable" mean?
It literally means a "comparison."

10. What are five things a parable does?
    1. It gives us a story.
    2. It gives us an ethical example.
    3. It teaches us something about the mind and heart of God.
    4. It is Christological.

Play the DVD - Disc 2, Segment 2

Talking it Out

Discussion Questions

1. Why does God honor fasting and why isn't it done more?
2. Do you think that Christ would choose *you* from among a group of disciples to be one of the ones He sent out, one of His apostles? Why or why not?
3. What talents or skills do you think are most necessary for an apostle?
4. Do you feel judged by the world? Do you feel judged by God? Explain.

Thinking it Through

Going back to the opening question, do you believe that God still works miracles, why or why not? If you could ask Jesus for one miracle, "big" or "small" (in your opinion), what would it be and why? Are you confident that He would respond according to His will? Do you think that His will lies in accordance with your plans? Why or why not?

Session 5
The Kingdom is at Hand

Opening Prayer

God our Father, thank you for the gift of the Church and for the tremendous gift of the Papacy and the sacramental priesthood. Let us never forget how much you love us, to entrust us and our spiritual care to these shepherds on earth. Holy Spirit, guardian and author of our Church, protect us from the darkness and untruths of sin that pervade our world. Call us to the truth. Call us to live always in the light of Christ. Call believers out of sin and sinners out of disbelief. May our time in this study, Lord, continue to build your Kingdom here on earth. Amen. *(Pray a Glory Be).*

Have you ever heard someone utter the following phrase, "I believe in God, I just don't believe in organized religion"? This is a popular misconception about religion–i.e., if it is "organized," then it must not be authentic or pure. Nothing could be further from the truth.

The Church didn't come from the Bible; the Bible came from the Church.

Think about that phrase for a minute. It's true. People often point to mistakes or past sins as reasons to reject religion. While humans are imperfect and sinful, the Church is perfect; it is divine, the bride of Christ, and perfect in its teaching. The Church, too, is made up of humans who are all touched by sin.

The Church is guided and protected by the Holy Spirit. In this session, you'll sit front row as the drama unfolds. Jesus Christ reveals not only His plan to build a Church, but also how He will build it and where His plan of salvation, brought to fruition through the Church, will take us.

The Chapters Covered in This Lesson

Matthew 16-17

Opening Question

How can we know if something is true?

Verse to Remember

Matthew 16:26 - "For what will it profit a man, if he gains the whole world and forfeits his life?"

Breaking it Down

1. What does the name Peter mean? 16:18
   It literally means "rock" or "stone."

1. What do the keys symbolize? (see Mt 16:19; Is 22:22)
   The keys symbolize authority.

2. What do verses 16-18 mean?
   Christ came to establish a church and give Peter authority

3. Why is Jesus so harsh with Peter (16:23)?
   Peter is not thinking as God thinks, he is thinking as man.

4. What does transfiguration mean?
   Transfiguration means a complete change in form to something elevated or more beautiful.

5. Where is the Transfiguration foreshadowed/prefigured?
   With Moses on Mt. Sinai (Exodus 34).

6. Who is present at the Transfiguration?
   Jesus, Moses, Elijah, Peter, James, and John.

7. What does the word "tent" translate to?
   Tent translates to "tabernacle."

8. What does the Transfiguration have to do with you, today?
   We who behold the glory of Jesus will be transfigured one day too in Salvation.

9. Why does Jesus get so upset about with the apostles (17:14-21)?
   They were given the power to heal in Jesus' name but didn't use it – a sin of omission.

Play the DVD - Disc 3, Segment 1

Talking it Out

Discussion Questions

1. What do you think would be the most challenging aspect of being pope?
2. Why would Jesus entrust the leadership of His Church to imperfect, sinful people?
3. Are you currently doing everything you are capable of doing for the service of God's Kingdom on earth? Why not? How could you do more? Offer a practical, actual example.

Thinking it Through

Journal or Essay questions

Why would Christ establish a Church, what practical reasons can you offer for such a decision? Why is it important to have one Church? Why is it so vital, on a practical level, that *truth* is objective and not subjective? What would it mean to faith, life and final judgment if there was no Church and there was no objective truth? What would happen?

Session 6
Who will enter the Kingdom?

Opening Prayer

Lord Jesus, Savior and Judge, open our eyes and shed light in our souls this day. Reveal to us all of those areas in our lives that are keeping us from sainthood. Show us, Lord, what You desire for us to change, that we may be more pleasing in your sight and more loving toward our family, at home and within the Church. Call us out of our sin, God, and forward to You. By your grace, help us to live lives worthy of the call we have received in You and from Your Church. Thank you for finding us worthy to participate in sharing the good news of Your Kingdom on earth. Mother Mary, please pray with us...(Pray a Hail Mary). Amen.

If you ask the people around you in the classroom or youth group, "Who wants to go to heaven?", every hand will probably go up. But if you ask the follow-up question, "Who is certain they will go to heaven?", most of the hands will go down.

Why are we so comfortable living with such an inconsistency?

Jesus is merciful, yes, but He is not a pushover. He doesn't play "word games" when it comes to salvation. In this session you will hear Jesus use some very strong words and imagery in His teachings. His greatest desire, as God, is to have His children back home with Him in heaven. He desires it so badly that He pays the ultimate price of His own life. He gives us every opportunity to enter into the Kingdom with Him.

The Chapters Covered in this Lesson

Matthew 18-25

Opening Question

If you were to die today, are you certain you would go to Heaven?

Verse to Remember

Matthew 22:14 - "For many are called, but few are chosen."

Breaking it Down

2. Who is the greatest in the Kingdom of Heaven? (see Mt 18:1-4)
   Those who are humble like children.

3. What must we do to enter the Kingdom?
   We have to become small. We must decrease so God can increase.

4. What is Jesus teaching us, practically, about purity (18:5-9)?
   Because sin isn't private. It affects and drags others down.

5. What is Jesus referring to in 18:18?
Reconciliation - the binding and loosing of sin.

6. Why Moses allow for divorce and Jesus say about it? (Mt 19:1-12)
Moses allowed for it to preserve life. Jesus says that at the beginning, in God's laws, marriage was an outward sign of God's love. There is no divorce. They shouldn't be fixated on Moses law, but God's law.

7. What do we learn from the Rich Young Man? (Mt 19:16-30)
He concentrated too much on merely external obedience.

8. Why is Jesus' entry into Jerusalem such a big deal? (Mt 20:29-21:17)
He is fulfilling a prophecy.

9. What does the wedding garment in Mt. 22 symbolize?
Righteousness; purity of a life lived for God.

10. What does hypocrite mean and who does Jesus say are hypocrites?
- A hypocrite is one who pretends to be something he or she is not.
- The Pharisees are called hypocrites by Jesus.

11. What is Jesus telling us about the end times? (Mt 24:1-35)
The old covenant is coming to an end and I am the new covenant.

Play the DVD - Disc 3, Segment 2

Talking it Out

Discussion Questions

1. Why is no sin truly private? In your own words, offer examples of sins people try to say are "private" that "hurt no one else" and explain how this idea is false.
2. What are the greatest assaults on purity? Give examples.
3. Why do so many people lead hypocritical lives? Why do we still struggle with hypocrisy even 2,000 years after Jesus called us out on the topic?

Thinking it Through

Journal or Essay questions

What does God want most **from** you? What does God want most **for** you? What are you basing your answers on, your own beliefs or on Scripture? Explain. What are some of the areas that you have changed in your life and faith that you can offer as proof that you are willing to embrace Christ's "new covenant"? What are those areas of your life that you are still fearful of surrendering to God?

Session 7
The King's earthly banquet and coronation

Opening Prayer

Holy Spirit, through the mystery of the Sacraments, You offer us the very body and blood of our Lord and Savior Jesus Christ. Today, open our eyes, our ears and our hearts in a new way, that we might embrace more deeply, the beauty of the Eucharist. Spirit, we thank You for Your enduring presence in our souls, our lives, our homes and our Church. Help us never to doubt Your love for us, nor the power that we have in You. Lord Jesus, may we be humble and bold enough to take You at Your Word, and may Your flesh and blood give us the strength we need to live in Your Kingdom, building it daily. Amen. *(Pray a Glory Be).*

If you go to Mass every Sunday and holy day of obligation, you will have heard the words of consecration more than 1,000 times by the time you reach adulthood.

Do these words from Scripture penetrate your heart or are they "lost" on you out of repetition?

Earlier in Matthew's gospel, Jesus warned us about babbling on in prayer (6:5-7). Likewise, we need to be mindful during prayer of what is happening, especially at Mass. The Second Vatican Council affirmed that we are called to "full, conscious, active participation" at Mass. In this session, you will be reminded not only of where the liturgy of the Eucharist comes from, but to whom and by whom it is offered.

Be sure to pay close attention to what the King is doing here, it will forever alter your perspective of the altar.

The Chapters Covered in this Lesson

Matthew 26-27

Opening question

Do you "give thanks" daily to God for what He did on the cross?

Verse to remember

Matthew 26:26 - "Now as they were eating, Jesus took bread, and bless, and broke it, and gave it to his disciples and said, 'Take, eat; this is my body.'"

Breaking it down

1. What is Passover? (Mt 26:1-5)
   It is the feast that commemorates God's delivery of His people out of slavery in Egypt.

2. What does the anointing of Jesus symbolize?
   She is preparing Jesus' body for burial.

3. How is *this* Passover meal so different than the others taking place?
There is no lamb mentioned because Jesus is the Passover Lamb.

4. Where are the words of consecration?
"Take, eat, this is my Body."

5. What does "Gethsemane" mean? (Mt 26:36)
Gethsemane means "the place of crushing."

6. What prayer is Jesus quoting in the Garden? (Mt 26:39)
The "Our Father"

7. What does "Barabbas" mean? (Mt 27:15-23)
Barabbas means "son of the father."

8. How was the King adorned for His banquet? (Mt 27:27-31)
A crown, robe, and reed: the earthly symbols of a king.

9. What do Jesus' words from the cross mean (27:46)?
"My God, my God, why have you forsaken me?"
The words come from the beginning of Psalm 22.

10. What is the significance of the torn veil in the temple?
The veil separated God from the people. Christ's death gives us access to the Father.

Play the DVD - Disc 4, Segment 1

Talking it Out

Discussion Questions

1. Why is the Eucharist so central to the Catholic faith?
2. Why would God desire for us to eat His flesh and drink His blood? Explain.
3. Why is it so important that St. Matthew recorded that scene of Jesus praying in the Garden of Gethsemane, when He is sorrowful, afraid and sweating blood?

Thinking it Through

Journal or Essay questions

Why is it so difficult for people to believe in Christ's Real Presence in the Eucharist? What are the most common objections? What would your answers be to those objections? What would God's answers be to those objections? What has to happen, in your opinion, for more people to believe that the bread and wine are actually Christ's body and blood?

Session 8
The Triumph of the King

Opening Prayer

Lord Jesus, in the truth of Your resurrection You fulfill Your promise to us of eternal life. Thank You, Lord, for what You did on the cross. Thank You, Jesus, for paying the price for our sins. Thank You for opening the door to everlasting life for us. Help us, dear Jesus, to live lives worthy of heaven. Help us, too, to remain focused on the vocations you put before us, to live holy and fruitful lives, until you call us home to the Heavenly Kingdom. Mother Mary, please pray with us, that we might offer our entire lives to the service of God, as You did. Amen. *(Pray a Hail Mary).*

Imagine if the story of Jesus Christ ended at the tomb. Imagine the consequences if there were no Resurrection: no redemption, no salvation, no heaven, no eternal life. It's too dark and too hopeless even to think about.

It's easy, though, to file away the resurrection as a "story you know" without examining the details. Pay close attention to what is happening in the final chapters of the gospel and in this final session. Matthew is using few words to say a great deal.

If you're now starting to think that you know all about Jesus in the gospels, think again. Yes, you know more, but you can never exhaust the Gospel of Jesus Christ. When this session ends, the real work and the real joy begins ... letting Jesus get to know you through His Word.

The Chapters Covered in this Lesson

Matthew 28

Opening Question

Does your life proclaim the resurrection of Jesus Christ?

Verse to Remember

Matthew 28:5 - "But the angel said to the women, "Do not be afraid; for I know that you seek Jesus who was crucified."

Breaking it Down

1. Who were the first witnesses of the Resurrection? (Mt 28:1)
   Mary Magdalene and the other Mary

2. What's the significance of Jesus' rising at dawn on the first day?
   It changes the traditional day of their worship.

3. Why is the truth of the resurrection so important?
Without the resurrection, we are still in our sins and without hope of heaven.

4. What does the "scheme" described in 28:11-15 demonstrate?
They are afraid of the truth of His resurrection.

5. Who is present at the commissioning?
The eleven remaining apostles.

6. Why did they go to the mountain?
Because Jesus told them to go to the mountain.

7. How does verse 28:17 gives us "hope" in our daily walk?
Because they doubted like we do - even after all they had seen. So there is hope for us.

8. What are the three things Jesus commands them to do?
- Make disciples of all the nations.
- Baptize them in the name of the Father, Son, and the Holy Spirit.
- Teach them to observe all that I have commanded you.

9. How does Jesus fulfill the promise He gives us in verse 20?
"I am always with you." He is eternally present in the Word and the Eucharist.

10. What name/title of Jesus does this promise refer back to?
Emmanuel meaning "God is with us."

Play the DVD - Disc 4, Segment 2

Talking it Out

Discussion Questions

1. Why isn't Easter a bigger deal to most modern believers? Why does Christmas get so much more attention?
2. How would you go about explaining the importance of Easter to someone who was Catholic but didn't think much of it? How about to an agnostic or atheist?
3. Do you believe that God is with **you**? Why or why not? What would need to happen for you to feel God's presence more intimately or for you to pray more, daily?

Thinking it Through

Journal or Essay questions

Are you open to whatever God calls you to do ... even if He were to call you to priesthood or religious life? Even if He called you to move away from loved ones? Even if He called you to poverty or to a life of service? Why or why not? How far are you willing to go for God and what areas are you most afraid of surrendering to Him? What percentage of your life is about building His Kingdom and what percentage is focused on your Kingdom? Apply percentages and explain.

Instructions for Thy Kingdom Come Optional Bible Studies

Note: As mentioned previously, the ten Optional Bible Studies included in this Leader's Guide are <u>not</u> found in the Student Workbook.

Opening Prayer

The prayers provided at the beginning of each study are based on the theme being discussed in the particular study. These prayers, of course, are optional, but be sure to make time to pray as a group prior to proclaiming the Scripture passage you will be studying.

Entering the Story

Choose someone ahead of time (maybe a week or so prior to the study) to proclaim the particular biblical passage you will be studying.

<u>Before</u> the opening prayer, ask the teens to open their Bibles to the specified passage. Have them mark the page or leave it open on their desks or laps. In this way, the passage will serve as a conclusion to the opening prayer rather than something done as a follow-up.

Have the appointed teen read the passage aloud, slowly and reverently, beginning and ending with the proper introduction to the book ("A reading from the gospel of St. Matthew") and salutation ("This is the Word of the Lord").

Breaking it Down

In this section, it is essential for teens to get the basic "lay of the land" within the story–the *who, what, when, where, why,* and *how* of the story. Encourage your students to read again silently the passage that was just proclaimed. Next, ask them the *who, what, when, where, why,* and *how* questions provided.

We have included all the basic facts of each study, but it is better to have the students answer the questions. Try to avoid jumping in if they get stuck on a particular question. Have them search their Bibles until they find the particular reference or answer. This will help them learn to navigate both their Bible and map of first century Palestine (in their study guides).

In "Breaking It Down," you will see the question, **"What are the details/words that jump out at you in this passage?"** This is a very important aspect of adolescent Scripture study. Different facts and details impact teens in different ways. Encourage them to read through the passage again and to look for words that strike them (e.g., action verbs, numbers, colors, details, names, facts, etc.), anything that jumps out to them, speaks to them, or confuses them. Once they have had an opportunity to read and reflect, allow them to share which words or passages struck them. Optimally, you will have a chalkboard, whiteboard, or smartboard that will allow you to record their responses and have them visible as you move through the study. Invariably, many of the things they alluded to will be covered in the following sections.

Pay particular attention to which teens are struck by which words. These responses will help you as leader to more helpfully discern how to keep the students interested by learning "where they are" on their faith journey.

"A Few More Questions to Ponder" gives you questions to ask the group. Each question is meant to flush out some of the more intriguing or confusing elements of the passage that was read. These answers will give the teens important insights into the stories and allow them to get "on the same page" as you move forward.

"A Few Things to Point Out" provides a little more background or context regarding certain elements within the particular passage. Without going so deep that the teens would lose interest, these brief exegetical notes about different elements within the passage provide teens with some interesting points. that are useful for taking your group deeper into the Sacred Scriptures.

Talking it Out

These discussion questions act as a bridge between the passage studied and the teens' everyday lives. They are intended to elicit discussion and reaction; some will provoke "simpler" answers while others will lead teens far deeper. Often, these are the questions that will require the greatest amount of guidance and pastoral direction on your part as leader.

Thinking it Through

This section functions as a great opportunity for the teens to internalize the truths being shared and find practical, tangible ways that the Scriptures will impact their daily faith walk. It can also be easily turned into a quality large group discussion, if your group is comfortable with one another and respectful, or it can be "massaged" into a more formalized essay question, within a classroom setting.

Additional Verses

These are optional verses that you can look up as a group, time permitting, or encourage the teens to look up on their own over the course of the week that follows. They are thematically based and (often) linked to the verses you've spent time studying within the study.

Closing Prayer

As with the opening prayer, the closing prayer provided is designed to point back to the truths presented in the study and to focus the teens' minds and hearts back to the theme one final time.

Bible Study 1

Duel in the Desert: The Temptation of Jesus

Opening Prayer

Let's take a moment and enter into the presence of God. (Pause for some silent time). *Lord Jesus, You know well the temptations of this world, yet You did not bow or yield to them. Open our eyes in this study of Your word, Lord, to more clearly see the temptations in our world that we so easily and so often succumb to and through the power of the Holy Spirit, grant us the strength we need to avoid them. Amen.*

Entering the Story

A reading from the gospel of St. Matthew...

Read Matthew 4:1-11

This is the Word of the Lord.

Breaking it Down

Who is involved? Jesus and Satan.
What is happening? The devil is trying to test Jesus and get Him to reveal His identity.
When does this take place? After Jesus' baptism and forty-day fast .
Where does this happen? In the desert/wilderness.
Why is this happening? It is preparing Jesus for His ministry.
How does this relate to the rest of the Gospel? Satan continues to look for opportunities to trip up and destroy Jesus.
What are the details/words that jump out at you in this passage? Possible examples: led by the Spirit, forty days, hungry, tempter, bread alone, parapet, Son of God, the test, kingdoms, prostrate, worship.

A Few More Questions to Ponder:

- Why would St. Matthew choose to include this scene of Jesus' life in his gospel? What do you think he was trying to get across to his readers?
- What character in the Old Testament do you remember fasting for forty days and nights? (Answer: Moses; see Exodus 24:18)
- What did Satan want from Jesus in exchange for "the world" in the third temptation?
- Which commandment does Jesus' third response mirror?

A Few Things to Point Out:

- Satan is trying to get Jesus to avoid suffering and/or death. Consider this in light of what Jesus says to St. Peter in **Matthew 16:23.**
- Both Jesus and Satan quote from Scripture. Just because someone quotes the Bible does not mean that they are using it to glorify God.
- The devil tries to persuade Jesus to use His power for Himself. We can never fall into that trap. Our gifts are entrusted to us for the service of the Church (see **1 Peter 4:10B**).

Talking it Out

1. *Why did Jesus head into the desert?* The Spirit led Him there to be tempted by the devil.
2. *What does this verse mean in relation to Hebrews 4:15-16?* Because Jesus knows what it is like to be tempted and because He was sinless and perfect in the face of those temptations, we should have confidence and can approach Him for grace, mercy and help in the face of our own temptations.
3. *What does Jesus' response of quoting the Scriptures teach us?* Jesus didn't need anything else for any response to the devil ... the Scriptures say more than enough in the face of temptations. He knew them. We should know them, too.
4. *What is the only non-Scriptural response that Jesus utters to the devil? What does that teach us?* We need only claim Jesus in the face of temptation and tell the devil to flee and he will flee.

Thinking it Through

Obviously, the devil strikes at Jesus when He was at His "weakest" (i.e., hungry after fasting for forty days). The devil knows our weaknesses, our Achilles' heels, so to speak, and he stops at nothing to exploit them.

Identify what areas in your life are your weaknesses, your "entry points" for the devil to tempt you. What can you do to eliminate them and offer them to God, in an effort to defend yourselves from the slings and arrows of the evil one?

Additional Verses:

Ephesians 6:16
2 Thessalonians 3:3
James 4:8-9
1 Peter 5:8

Closing Prayer

Close with the St. Michael Prayer

St. Michael the Archangel, defend us in battle. Be our protection against the wickedness and snares of the Devil. May God rebuke him, we humbly pray, and do thou, O Prince of the heavenly hosts, by the power of God, thrust into hell Satan and all the evil spirits who prowl about the world seeking the ruin of souls. Amen.

Bible Study 2

Attitude Adjustment: The Beatitudes

Opening Prayer

God our Father, you call us to new life. You call us to live a life that is in perfect harmony with your will. Help us to think more of others than we do of ourselves. Mother Mary, be a Mother to us now. Hold us close to you. Pray with us and for us, that we, too, might be seen as "blessed" in the eyes of our Heavenly Father. Join Your Immaculate prayers to ours as we focus on Your Son. Amen. (Pray a Hail Mary).

Entering the Story

A reading from the gospel of St. Matthew...

Read Matthew 5:3-12

This is the Word of the Lord.

Breaking it Down

Who is involved? Jesus, His disciples, and the crowds.
What is happening? He is comforting the afflicted and afflicting the comfortable.
When does this take place? At the beginning of His ministry, after He calls the first apostles.
Where does this happen? Up north, in Galilee
Why is this happening? Jesus is educating the crowd and changing their perspective
How does this relate to the rest of the Gospel?
What are the details/words that jump out at you in this passage? Possible examples: the mountain, blessed, poor in spirit, mourn, meek, hunger, mercy, clean of heart, peacemakers, persecuted, righteousness, falsely, reward, kingdom.

A Few More Questions to Ponder:

- What would be the advantage to offering this teaching in this more poetic style for people who didn't have anything to write on, or who, perhaps, could not even read?
- Did you notice how each beatitude builds on the one preceding it?
- If you look at the rest of chapter five, you will notice that Christ begins with the Beatitudes, redefining who is truly blessed and how we are to live, prior to teaching how we are **not** to live. Why do you think He would present these truths in that order?
- What is the significance of Christ being on "the mountain" as He gives this teaching? What other significant things occur on a mountain in Scripture?

A Few Things to Point Out:

- The first seven Beatitudes (5:3-9) mirror the seven gifts of the Holy Spirit
- In the Psalms, those who are *blessed* include: those whose sins are forgiven, those who are part of God's family, those who love God and those who participate in His life.
- The structure of "they shall" points to a heavenly reward for earthly trials, making each beatitude a divine promise, of sorts.

- Notice what verse 3 and verse 10 promises ... what is heaven likened to? (A particularly important point for *Thy Kingdom Come.*)

Talking it Out

What does it mean to be "poor in spirit"? It means those who are truly aware of the need for God's mercy. Additionally, it is for those without possessions, whose sole reliance is on God.

1. *What is righteousness?* It means living your life in conformity to the will of God ... essentially, that your will and God's will are consistent and one.
2. *Why is the allusion to the last line, regarding the prophets' persecution, included? Wouldn't the assurance of persecution be a motivating factor not to live this way?* The prophets were chosen by God and were heroic, held in high esteem. Additionally, Christ is calling us to embrace worldly suffering, trusting in the heavenly promise.

Thinking it Through

If you learned, remembered and lived out the beatitudes in your daily life, what difference would it make? How would your attitude change? How would your life change? Would it make a difference in your home environment? In your school or work environment? Within your circle of friends, would it make a difference?

Additional Verses:

Psalm 37:11
Luke 1:48
Colossians 3:12
James 2:13
1 Peter 2:20
Revelation 21:4

Closing Prayer

Pray through each of the Beatitudes in order, asking God to grant you the courage or grace to live out each one.

Here are a couple of examples:

"God our Father, give us the courage to put our trust in You and to live our lives poor in spirit..."

"Lord Jesus, give us the grace we need to lean into You when we are in mourning..."

Bible Study 3

Jesus: the Bible's First Real Estate Agent – Two Foundations

Opening Prayer

Lord Jesus, you love us enough to warn us of worldly dangers and distractions. You love us enough, Lord, that You stop at nothing to give us every opportunity at Heaven. Shake us free from our shortsightedness and pride this day, Jesus. Shed your divine light in our souls and illuminate in us all that we need to change, to live more securely in You. Help us to pray to your Father with confidence as You did, trusting that He is working constantly for our salvation. Amen. (Pray an Our Father)

Entering the Story

A reading from the gospel of St. Matthew...

Read Matthew 7:24-29

This is the Word of the Lord.

Breaking it Down

Who is involved? Jesus and the crowds
What is happening? Jesus is offering wisdom about how to live our life.
When does this take place? This dialogue is placed within the Sermon on the Mount.
Where does this happen? On a small mountain in Galilee, possibly in Chorazin.
Why is this happening? Jesus is teaching and giving new perspective on the Kingdom.
How does this relate to the rest of the Gospel? Jesus is calling people to a new Covenant.
What are the details/words that jump out at you in this passage? Possible examples: everyone, acts, wise man, rock, rain, floods, winds, collapse, solidly, fool, sand, ruined, astonished, authority

A Few More Questions to Ponder:

- Does an analogy of building your own house mean much to us in the modern, civilized world? Did you build your own house? Do you think it meant more to them, in the ancient world?
- What would be a more modern analogy that you could use for this teaching?
- Who is the "fool" described as is in Jesus' words? (Answer: the one who listens to His words but does not act on them.)

A Few Things to Point Out:

- Who does "everyone who listens" refer to? That's right, everyone–every Christian, not just those who are disciples but those, too, in leadership–the learned and the ignorant are all subject to this same teaching
- The wise man Jesus is alluding to is King Solomon (whom you might remember from *T3:The Teen Timeline* and his building of God's house (the Temple) in **1 Kings 3:10; 8:27**.
- Notice that this teaching based on those who "hear and do," but the teachings that proceed it (verses 15-23) are based upon those who "say and do."
- The house is also the soul: built on Christ it will last, built on worldly treasure it will be swept away

Talking it Out

What would an example of the Rock be that we, as Catholics, build our "houses" upon? See **Matthew 16:18**.

1. *God's Word demands a response from us. What are the pros and cons of building your house on each of the foundations?* The pro of building on sand is that it costs less, is easier and more "timely." The con is that it doesn't last. Building on rock is more difficult, more costly and take more time, but it stands forever.
2. *Why were the crowds so astonished at His teachings?* He taught with authority and not as a scribe, meaning that the scribes were teaching "old, existent traditions and teachings" but Jesus was teaching something new with a voice of authority, like Moses.

Thinking it Through

Shifting sand is an analogy for all of the ever-changing "things" of the world that you cannot put your faith in: wealth, popularity, looks, material possessions, etc. What do you have that cannot be taken away? What do you desire that cannot be taken away, will not break, age or be without value months or years from now? **Read and write out Isaiah 40:8** and **1 Corinthians 13:9-10, 13**, and discuss (or journal about) them.

Additional Verses:

Psalm 127:1
Proverbs 10:25
Isaiah 26:4
Isaiah 28:16
Matthew 21:42
Mark 1:22
1 Corinthians 3:11
1 Peter 2:6-7

Closing Prayer

Ask a teen to lead a closing prayer, focusing on all of those "rocks" that God gives us, sturdy people (family, leaders, priests, papacy) that guide us and sturdy "things" (the Bible, Church teaching, the sacraments) that support our walk with Christ.

BIBLE STUDY 4

FAMILY FEUD: A CAUSE OF DIVISION

OPENING PRAYER

Mother Mary, we thank you for the example that You are to us and for the surrender that You exemplify and call us to live. Pray for us now, Blessed Mother, that we can be more loving children and more obedient followers of Your Son, Jesus. St. Joseph, pray for us, so that we can humbly and courageously seek and live a holy life as you did. Join your prayers to ours that our families would be holy families as yours is, and that our households would resemble houses of worship, where we focus more on Your Son than on the stresses and sins of the day. We pray that our families would glorify You, Jesus. Amen. (Pray a Glory Be).

ENTERING THE STORY

A reading from the gospel of St. Matthew...

Read Matthew 10:34-39

This is the Word of the Lord.

BREAKING IT DOWN

Who is involved? Jesus and the twelve apostles.
What is happening? Jesus is giving them instructions as He sends them out on a mission.
When does this take place? During Jesus' public ministry.
Where does this happen? In Galilee.
Why is this happening? To teach that God must come first.
How does this relate to the rest of the Gospel? It reminds us that some will reject the Kingdom ... and still do.
What are the details/words that jump out at you in this passage? Possible examples: peace, sword, father, mother, enemies, household, loves, worthy, cross, loses his life.

A Few More Questions to Ponder:

- Why would Jesus include this "negative" type of passage in the middle of commissioning His apostles to go out and heal? Shouldn't He keep it positive?
- Obviously Jesus didn't carry a sword, so why the imagery of the sword?
- Although crucifixion was a widespread and popular form of punishment at this time, Jesus (obviously) had not yet been crucified. What do you think the apostles were thinking when Jesus uttered this phrase about "taking up their cross"?
- What does it mean to "lose your life" in order to find it?

A Few Things to Point Out:

- Notice that Jesus is very upfront with what following Him entails: self-denial and suffering ... possibly even death. He doesn't try to "trick you" into following Him with promises of earthly wealth of glory; there is no "fine print" in Jesus' call.
- As your life becomes more in line with the life of Christ, as His light "burns brighter in you" the darkness around you becomes more apparent, as do the faces of those who are immersed in it - even family.

- This passage notes that we will share in the cross of Christ ... which presupposes (since we know "how the story ends") that we will also share in the resurrection and victory.
- The truth of Christ and the cross of Christ both create a division in "believers," those who say they believe and those who prove it in their actions. Ironically, it is only through that division that we actually achieve any unity.

Talking it Out

Does Jesus desire conflict within your family? No, Jesus desires peace (**Read John 10:10, 16:33**), and He knows the only way you will achieve it is for you to abandon your will and live in God's will.

1. *What is Jesus telling us about the importance of our relationship with our Heavenly Father?* That it is primary, even more primary than our relationship with our earthly father/mother.
2. *Notice that God does not allow for any household to be forgotten, He is acting for the salvation of all. Who in your household or family tree has God sent as an example of faith for the rest?*
3. *How does Christ judge our worthiness in this passage?* Our worthiness is based upon our willingness to suffer. Note that it doesn't say we have to "enjoy" the suffering, only that we are willing to endure it, trusting in His promise.

Thinking it Through

Does your faith walk draw your family and friends closer to Jesus or create conflict in your life? Is God using you to bring your family back to Him, through your openness and example or does your family point and lead you into a deeper relationship with Him? Given your answer to these previous questions, what is your prayer this day, one of hope for your loved ones or one of thanksgiving for them? Explain.

Additional Verses:

Matthew 16:24-25
Luke 1:46-48, 9:23 (note the word "daily")
John 12:25
Ephesians 6:17

Closing Prayer

Today, as we close in prayer, let's reflect on the words of the saints.

St. Anselm once wrote these words about Jesus, our Savior:

> He is crowned, but His crown is a torture to Him and wounds with a thousand punctures, His most glorious head. He is clothed in royal purple; yet more despised than honored in it. He bears a scepter in hand, but with it His reverend head is beaten. They worship before Him with bowed knee; they hail Him king: while they leap up to spit upon His cheeks ... they smite His jaws with the palms of their hands ... He is constrained, spit upon, despised.

Lord, Jesus, thank you for loving us. Help us to love you with the same disregard for self. Help us to become more selfless, Lord, that we might embrace our earthly crosses, each day.

Help us to understand these words from St. John Vianney:

> You must accept your cross; if you carry it courageously it will carry you to heaven. God commands you to pray, but He forbids you to worry.

Bible Study 5

When the Carpenter Becomes the Farmer: Sower and Seed

Opening Prayer

Holy Spirit, open our hearts to receive the Word of God this day. Open our eyes to see what You intended for us to see when You inspired these words. Open our ears to hear the truth of God. Open our souls so that the seed of God's Word would find rich and fertile soil. And open our mouths, Holy Spirit, that we might share the good news God gives us daily. (Pray the following prayer three times) Come Holy Spirit, fill the hearts of your faithful and enkindle in us the fire of your love. Amen.

Entering the Story

A reading from the gospel of St. Matthew...

Read Matthew 13:1-9

This is the Word of the Lord.

Breaking it Down

Who is involved? Jesus and the crowds.
What is happening? Jesus is teaching through parables.
When does this take place? During Jesus' public ministry.
Where does this happen? Up north, in Galilee.
Why is this happening? To give insight into the mystery of the Kingdom.
How does this relate to the rest of the Gospel? Jesus came to announce the Kingdom.
What are the details/words that jump out at you in this passage? Possible examples: on that day, by the sea, large crowds, the shore, at length, sower, seed, path, rocky ground, soil, not deep, scorched, withered, thorns, choked, fruit.

A Few More Questions to Ponder:

- Did you notice the detail in Matthew 13:1? Did you notice the small details about Jesus "going out of the house"? Is that detail relevant to the story? Why would it be included? (Answer: it ties it to the previous episode, yes, but it also gives us the insight into the author as an eyewitness)
- How does the detail discussed above relate to this story in chapter 13, and Matthew's call in chapter 9? (Answer: it happens after Matthew's call, giving us greater confidence that Matthew was witnessing these things, firsthand).
- Why is this parable the first or "foundational" parable? In other words, why does understanding this parable make it easier to understand all that come after it?
- What is the purpose of parables? (Hint: spend time reading verses 10 - 15 after discussing this question.)

A Few Things to Point Out:

- You might want to go back to the *Thy Kingdom Come* DVD set, and play the clip at the end of Session 4 (disc two), that discusses and gives an overview of parables.
- Sowing precedes plowing in the agricultural process and although not all of the seed bears fruit,

that which finds rich soil bears tremendous fruit. This foreshadows Jesus' message which will fall largely on deaf ears but which will also find rich soil in the hearts of many, a message that has literally transformed the world and survived for 2,000 years.

- Note where the distractions come from in the parable: the devil (verse 19), the flesh (verse 21) and the world (verse 22, 24).
- Parables disguise heavenly truths and mysteries in earthly situations, they shroud the divine in human terms.

Talking it Out

Spend time reading through verses 18-23 and discuss Jesus' explanation of the parable. Did the group discern the truths espoused within it, correctly?

1. *What are the four "destinations" or "types of persons" that receive the seed (Word)?*
    - Those who never accept the word or kingdom
    - Those who believe for awhile but fall away, for lack of roots
    - Those who believe but "choke" on worldly fears/anxieties and material seductions
    - Those who receive it with an open heart and bear fruit
2. *Does Christ intend this parable only for the ignorant masses or for those who are great sinners?* No, as verse nine affirms, this is a reminder for everyone. We cannot fall into the trap of thinking that this doesn't apply to us or that "we're too holy". That belief hardens the soil of the human heart.

Thinking it Through

What are the things that harden the soil of your heart? What situations or relationships make it difficult for you to accept God's Word? What situations or relationships pull you away from your faith walk or prayer life? What fears, anxieties and desires lure you into sin or cause you to turn your back on totally surrendering to God? What things can you proactively do to insure that the soil of your heart is rich and fertile, tilled and ready to receive?

Additional Verses:

Galatians 5:22-23
John 15:5
Jeremiah 17:10
Psalm 1:1-3
Genesis 1:11
James 5:7, 18
Colossians 1:10

Closing Prayer

Write out the four "types" of soil on the board. As you close in prayer, point out and pause for a solid minute of silence at each "type," asking the teens to offer up to God in prayer all those in their life who they feel fall into each "soil" category. Tell them to include themselves in one of the categories while they pray, too, asking the Lord to grant them Divine assistance in tilling their soil until it is fertile and open to the seed of God's word.

Bible Study 6

God has More Patience than a Hospital: The Weeds and Wheat

Opening Prayer

God our Father, thank you for looking through our unworthiness and finding worth. Lord Jesus Christ, by the blood You shed on the cross for us, You make us worthy, You reconcile us to the Father. Thank you for your love and Your mercy. Holy Spirit, You call us to new life, to leave behind the ways of the world and embrace the call to holiness, to chastity, to purity and to service. Grant us the strength we need to live out that call to sainthood, each day. May all we do in the time together, glorify You, God. (Pray a Glory Be.)

Entering the Story

A reading from the gospel of St. Matthew...

Read Matthew 13:24-30

This is the Word of the Lord.

Breaking it Down

Who is involved? Jesus and the crowds.
What is happening? Jesus is teaching through parables.
When does this take place? During Jesus' public ministry.
Where does this happen? Up north, in Galilee.
Why is this happening? To give insight into the mystery of the Kingdom.
How does this relate to the rest of the Gospel? Jesus came to announce the Kingdom.
What are the details/words that jump out at you in this passage? Possible examples: proposed, kingdom, good seed, asleep, enemy, weeds, wheat, bore fruit, slaves, Master, pull them up, together, harvest time, burning, barn.

A Few More Questions to Ponder:

- What do you think this parable means? What is it about?
- Why does Jesus choose to use so many farming, agricultural references in His parables?
- Could you discern the difference between weeds and wheat? Can the average person? What about the people listening to Jesus who couldn't tell the difference? Does this parable mean nothing to them? Did Jesus stop to think about that? Explain.
- What is "harvest time"? What is the fire (for burning) and what is the barn?

A Few Things to Point Out:

- Young people who are not familiar with gardening need to understand a fundamental truth: if the weeds are uprooted too soon, the wheat is endangered.
- The weeds signify the enemy (i.e., Satan) and the work of his hands.
- Certain plants (e.g., darnel, a poisonous weed) look like wheat in their early stages but must be left to mature until the gardener can be sure. In some cases, only time tells if something (or someone)

will produce fruit or be dangerous to the plants that bear fruit/life.
- In our humanity we may long for the day that all the weeds (evil) will be gathered and destroyed (judgment), but we must be patient and trust in God's timing.

Talking it Out

What is Jesus warning His disciples about in this parable? He is warning them not to be too quick to judge others or to be "too sure" about whether or not they have a place in the Kingdom.

1. *Why is this parable good news for us, as sinners, and for those sinful souls whom we love?* It is not too late. Every day is a new opportunity to turn your heart back to God and give your life to Jesus.
2. *Utilizing verses 36-43, unpack this parable through the words of Christ.*

Thinking it Through

How can you discern the difference between weeds and wheat in your own life? Which people around you are weeds, threatening your spiritual well-being? Which people around you are wheat, "bearing fruit" and bringing life? Which are you called to be and what are you called to do?

Additional Verses:

Job 31:40
Psalm 72:16
Luke 15:7, 10
James 5:19-20
1 Peter 4:8
1 John 3:10

Closing Prayer

Spend time praying aloud as a group, offering petitions for family members or friends who might be seriously ill or who are facing struggles in their lives. Before you pray, pick one or two teen leaders to begin and end the prayer.

Bible Study 7

A Pirate's Favorite Parable: Buried Treasure

Opening Prayer

God our Father, help us to see the beauty of Your Son, Jesus Christ, more clearly. Unearth in us the desire, to abandon all we have and all we know to follow Your Son more closely. Holy Spirit, take us to new depths in our relationship with Jesus, our Savior, and pour out Your grace upon us so that we would have the courage to live for Him daily. Lord Jesus, pray with us now, that we might live more perfectly in Your image. Amen. (Pray an Our Father).

Entering the Story

A reading from the gospel of St. Matthew...

Read Matthew 13:44-50

This is the Word of the Lord.

Breaking it Down

Who is involved? Jesus and the crowds.
What is happening? Jesus is teaching through parables.
When does this take place? During Jesus' public ministry.
Where does this happen? Up north, in Galilee.
Why is this happening? To give insight into the mystery of the Kingdom.
How does this relate to the rest of the Gospel? Jesus came to announce the Kingdom.
What are the details/words that jump out at you in this passage? Possible examples: kingdom, treasure, buried, finds and hides, joyfully, sells all, fine pearls, pearl of great price, net, throw away, separate, wicked, righteous, furnace, wailing, and grinding of teeth.

A Few More Questions to Ponder:

- Imagine that you are the main character in each of these parables, i.e., you are the landowner, the pearl merchant, and the fisherman/net. Each situation requires action on the main characters' part. What are you actively doing to grow in your faith life and prayer life, right now?
- Are you willing to undergo inconveniences and risk poverty to have Christ ("the treasure") in your "possession" (life)?
- Do you normally search for Christ like the merchant searches for pearls, or do you usually wait for Jesus to come to you? Discuss.
- What is the criteria fishermen use for separating good and bad fish? What do you think is God's criteria for separating the good and bad "fish" (i.e., people)?

A Few Things to Point Out:

- Notice that the principle character does not obtain the treasure or pearl out of his savings or wealth, he can only gain the treasure *after* selling all that they have to acquire it.
- In Greek, the letter *Chi* looks like an "X" in English. *Chi* is used to spell "Christ." Christ is the treasure in both these parables so, literally, "X" does mark the spot on this Scriptural treasure map.

- In New Testament times, it was a common practice in the Mediterranean world to bury one's valuables in the ground, given how rampant thieving and looting were and how drastic taxation had become.
- The poverty of the main character can be considered literal or spiritual (**Re-read Matthew 5:3**).

Talking it Out

The first parable about buried treasure states that the man has "great joy" as he sells his earthly things to obtain the field. Do you joyfully renounce worldliness to follow Jesus or do so begrudgingly? If we are honest with ourselves, the more truthful answer is that we give up worldly ways with some reluctance.

1. *What is the difference between counting the cost and calculating the cost (of following Jesus)?* When you count the cost you focus on all it is costing you and all you are having to give up to get it, when you calculate the cost you are thinking through the breadth of your sacrifice so as to make an informed, abandoned decision for the betterment of your soul. Counting leads to bitterness, calculating leads to success and freedom.
2. *If knowing Jesus and serving Him are the greatest treasure, why don't more people do both?* Explain how your answer ties back into **Matthew 6:21**.
3. *Is the imagery of the furnace, the separation and the wailing/grinding a motivator for you to change, personally or not?*

Thinking it Through

How "real" is the promise of eternal life to you? Is it real enough to sacrifice real, tangible things? Would you give up your iPod for the promise? How about your cell phone? How about your video game console, your computer or your closet of clothes? Would you give up your car? Your college savings? Would you give up everything for heaven? Why or why not? What, if anything, are you not willing to part with?

Additional Verses:

Deuteronomy 28:12
Tobit 4:9
Sirach 6:14
Matthew 6:21
2 Corinthians 4:7
Philippians 3:8
1 Timothy 6:19
James 5:3

Closing Prayer

Put on some instrumental music for about ten minutes and let the teens flip through the gospel of Matthew. Tell them that there is no specific verse or passage that they have to look up. Give them the opportunity for God to speak something new and personal to them through His living word. Let them flip around until they discover the treasure God wants to give to them this day. Instruct them that once they find the one verse or passage they feel God is really pointing them toward, have them mark the place in their Bible, reflect on it, and re-read it, pray about it, or journal about it until the time is up.

End with a prayer of thanksgiving for the time you spent studying for studying God's word.

Bible Study 8

The Dangers of Short-Term Memory: The Unforgiving Servant

Opening Prayer

Forgive me, Father ... Forgive me for all the ways that I put other relationships before You. Forgive me for all the times I take your name in vain or fail to pray. Forgive me, Father, for all the times I don't love others as I should love You or love myself as You love me. Forgive me for the ways I don't act as Your child. Forgive me for all the ways I take my eyes off of You or allow worldly, imperfect, material things to steal the attention and affection I should reserve only for You, God. Forgive me, Lord. Amen. (Pray an Our Father).

Entering the Story

A reading from the gospel of St. Matthew...

Read Matthew 18:21-35

This is the Word of the Lord.

Breaking it Down

Who is involved? Jesus, Peter, and the rest of the disciples.
What is happening? Jesus is clarifying His teaching about forgiveness.
When does this take place? After the Transfiguration, before He enters Jerusalem.
Where does this happen? In Galilee.
Why is this happening? To give insight into the mystery of the Kingdom.
How does this relate to the rest of the Gospel? Jesus is further clarifying life in the new Kingdom.
What are the details/words that jump out at you in this passage? Possible examples: How often must I, forgive, seven, seventy seven, kingdom of heaven, king, servants, debtor, huge amount, sold, compassion, choke him, begged, disturbed, wicked, pity, torturers, from his heart.

A Few More Questions to Ponder:

- In your opinion, why do we as humans want the exact number of times we are supposed to forgive? Why do we want to apply that limit to mercy when we have been wronged?
- How does it jeopardize us if God were to put a limit on mercy?
- The passage says that the Master was" moved with compassion." What has been your experience of people when you owe them something (i.e., money or a favor)? Are others compassionate with you when you are in their debt?
- How compassionate are you towards people who are indebted to you in some way? Do you ever take advantage of people because of any power or influence you have over them? (You might want to steer the conversations to include roles of leadership at work, on teams or within school. Additionally, you might want to mention roles at home, like that of an older sibling.)

A Few Things to Point Out:

- Jesus, of course, is not putting a limit (i.e., "seventy-seven") on how many times were are to forgive. This number is meant to evoke the idea of "without limit." Peter was looking for the letter of the law, Jesus was giving the spirit of it.

- The idea of "paying it back in full" (verse 26) is probably intended to be seen as an empty promise based upon the huge size of the debt mentioned here (6,000 denarii or twenty years of wages).
- Notice that it is Peter who asks Jesus the question. No other apostle is listed by name in this passage. It is significant that Peter is asking Jesus about forgiveness when it is Peter who seeks such forgiveness from our Lord following His passion.

Talking it Out

This concept of forgiveness is not a new one in the Gospel. Jesus gives us a similar teaching earlier in St. Matthew's gospel. Can you remember where? **Read Matthew 6:14-15.**

1. *Is Jesus saying that sins against us are not a big deal?* No, this is not to be misunderstood as Jesus just "sweeping wrongs against you under the rug." What Jesus is articulating is that, in comparison to our sins against God, others' offenses against us are insignificant.
2. *Did you notice "how" you are to forgive your brother (in verse 35)? How does the stipulation "from his heart" change the commandment?* If you've ever said "sorry" for hitting your sibling because Mom or Dad stood in front of you and made you do it, but you really had no sorrow for the action, you understand the difference. This forgiveness goes far deeper than words. This forgiveness must be authentic and rooted in humility.
3. *Refusing to forgive someone else is equivalent to refusing God's mercy towards ourselves.* Ponder this truth.

Thinking it Through

Do you hold others to a higher standard than you hold yourself? Do you get angry when other people like your parents "don't listen to you" as you, in turn, refuse to listen to them? Have you ever desired forgiveness without being willing to forgive someone whom you hold a grudge against?

Identify the relationships in your life that would change for the better if you were more humble ... before you point out what others need to change, spend some time in prayer asking God to reveal to you what you need to change in these relationships, first.

Additional Verses:

Psalm 72:13
Matthew 7:3-5, 19:19, 22:39
Romans 14:15, 21
Ephesians 4:2
Colossians 3:13
James 2:8

Closing Prayer

As a closing prayer exercise, give each teen a piece of blank paper and encourage them to write a letter asking forgiveness for someone they have hurt in the past week or month. If they say they "just can't think of anyone," then have them write a letter to God asking forgiveness for the times they have not loved as they should.

Close by praying an Our Father, taking time to really stress the final lines in which we beseech God for forgiveness.

Bible Study 9

There are Some Thing Money Can't Buy: The Rich Young Man

Opening Prayer

Lord God, you are so generous. You can never be outdone in generosity. We can never out-give you, God. With that truth in upon our hearts we come before You today, God, to say thank You for Your generosity. Thank you for all of the ways that You bless us even though we don't deserve it. We come before you, once again, asking that You would pour out Your grace on us and shower us with the riches of Your mercy. Amen. (Pray a Glory Be).

Entering the Story

A reading from the gospel of St. Matthew...

Read Matthew 9:16-30

This is the Word of the Lord.

Breaking it Down

Who is involved? Jesus, the young man, Peter, and the disciples.
What is happening? Jesus is clarifying the New Covenant laws.
When does this take place? Before Jesus enters into Jerusalem for the final time.
Where does this happen? In Judea.
Why is this happening? The young man wants to be justified and seeks clarification.
How does this relate to the rest of the Gospel? This instance is an example of the larger gospel message, helping the Jews to re-envision faithfulness, the moral life and salvation.
What are the details/words that jump out at you in this passage? Possible examples: teacher, eternal life, commandments, perfect, poor, treasure, follow me, many possessions, camel, needle, astonished, saved, impossible, throne of glory, first and last.

A Few More Questions to Ponder:

- Can you earn your way into heaven? (Hint: this is a great opportunity to discuss the difference between faith and works and the function of grace as God's free gift.)
- The young man is often viewed negatively for his response, but the truth is that he was authentic and honest and that he knew the commandments. Do you know the commandments?
- Is Jesus saying that rich people aren't in heaven? (Answer: No. Jesus does not say that wealth per se is evil but that the rich often hoard it or struggle more with trusting God than those with nothing. The *love* of money is evil – see 1 Timothy 6:10, Hebrews 13:5.)
- Is Peter doubting what they have sacrificed and second-guessing his decision? Why is he asking the question? Why don't the other apostles ask Jesus the question, do you think?
- The world is pretty selfish, often times, with everyone looking out for themselves. In what ways do you see or experience the truth "the first shall be last and the last shall be first"?

A Few Things to Point Out:

- This is yet another example of a teaching that unpacks further (and points back to) the core truths Jesus espoused in the Beatitudes, particularly (Matthew 5:3).
- The refusal of the young man to sell his possessions and embrace true physical poverty actually, ironically, proved Jesus' whole point.
- The "new age" (mentioned in verse 28) is a new beginning, a rebirth that comes with the ushering in of the New Kingdom.
- In the imagery of Jesus and the apostles on the thrones, it is a foreshadowing of the final judgment. If Jesus is saying that the apostles will join Jesus for the judgment, what does that say about the Church's apostolic authority and the right to "bind and loose" as we spoke about in Session 5, regarding authority?

Talking it Out

Is Jesus asking "too much" when He asks the young man to sell all of his possessions? Why or why not?

1. *What does Jesus' response tell us about the commandments? Is it "enough" just to keep the commandments in our daily life or does this New Covenant require something more from us?*
2. *Is the young man being told to follow the commandments, to follow Jesus or both?* (Answer: the young man is being given insight into the New Covenant/Kingdom. To be part of the new Kingdom, we must follow Christ in all ways–even in how He fulfills the commandments. Just obeying the commandments does not "fulfill" their intention).
3. *Do you think more people, like the Rich Young Man, would follow Jesus if it were easier? If so, than why doesn't God make it "easier" to follow Him?*

Thinking it Through

What areas of your life do you still hold onto, refusing to surrender them to God? Is God the God of your future? Where do you see yourself in five or ten years? Is that vision of your future self the product of prayer and discernment of God's will, or a product of personal plans and dreams, without God's input?

Additional Verses:

Psalms 112:19
Proverbs 21:13
2 Corinthians 9:9
1 Timothy 6:9-10
Hebrews 13:5
James 5:1-6

Closing Prayer

For closing in prayer, lead the teens through the following prayerful meditation:

Heavenly Father, open our eyes now...
Open our eyes to all of those things we hold onto tighter than You (pause for a few moments)
Open our eyes to all the worldly things that occupy our thoughts more than You (pause)
Open our eyes to all of those things we do out of fear and not out of love (pause)
Open our eyes, God, to all of those areas of our lives we push You out of (pause)
Help us, Father, to let you be God
Help us, Jesus, to follow you more closely
Help us, Spirit, to surrender our lives to your direction.
Pray three Hail Marys for greater surrender

Bible Study 10

"In What I Have Done and in What I Have Failed to Do": Sins of Commission vs. Omission

Opening Prayer

God our Father, You created us in Your divine image and likeness. You formed us in our mothers' wombs and consecrated us. You brought us to life with a specific vocation in Your mind, God, a vocation that only we can fulfill, Lord, through your grace. Every talent, every skill, every ability Lord is a gift from You, to be used for the building of Your Kingdom on earth and for Your glory. Help us to see more clearly those gifts You've bestowed upon us, God, and grant us the strength we need to put them into action each day, for the service of Your Church. Amen. (Pray a Hail Mary and a Glory Be).

Entering the Story

A reading from the gospel of St. Matthew...

Read Matthew 25:14-30

This is the Word of the Lord.

Breaking it Down

Who is involved? Jesus and His disciples.
What is happening? He is teaching about God's gifts and their purpose.
When does this take place? Just before the Passion of Christ.
Where does this happen? In Jerusalem.
Why is this happening? He is empowering His disciples, with an important reminder.
How does this relate to the rest of the Gospel? Their role is to actively seek the Kingdom.
What are the details/words that jump out at you in this passage? Possible examples: talents, buried, servants, Master, faithful, joy, responsibilities, wicked, lazy, scatter, bank, rich, useless, darkness, wailing, grinding.

A Few More Questions to Ponder:

- Have you ever thought of laziness as a sin? Why or why not? Explain how God can consider the failure to use the talents (i.e., the gifts He has entrusted to us) as a sin.
- What are the talents that God has entrusted to you? List several.
- Do you think most Catholics are more concerned with sins of commission or sins of omission?
- What about the sins of commission? How does Jesus deal with them? (Mercifully)
    - Woman caught in adultery – John 8:1-11
    - Peter's denial – John 18:15-17
    - Even with Judas – Luke 22:47-56
- Now, look at how he deals with Jesus in sins of omission. (Strongly)
    - Not feeding the hungry – Matthew 25:31- 46
    - Burying the talents – Matthew 25:14-30
    - Epileptic son – Luke 9:37-45

A Few Things to Point Out:

- A talent is a coin worth a sizable sum of money.
- Notice that the talents were wasted out of laziness (the deadly sin of sloth), in verses 26-28) and fear, in verse 25. Isn't that still the case, today?
- The servant who received the least was probably upset that the Master didn't trust him with more, so his actions (burying the talent) were more reactive than proactive.
- Talents, like muscles, will be lost if unused.
- The "journey" mentioned here is mirrored (in salvation history) as the time that takes place between Jesus' ascension and the final judgment.

Talking it Out

1. *List some sins of omission in your lives.*
   (Here are a few examples to prompt if the teens are quiet).

- Not thanking God
- Not praying
- Not going to Mass
- Not evangelizing
- Not serving others
- Not tithing
- Never fighting for justice
- Not speaking the truth of Christ
- Not fighting against abortion
- Not being courageous enough to give holy advice
- Not working hard, even when you get paid

2. Some would argue that burying the talents was the "safer move" and that the Master would have been mad if the money had been lost. *Does God want you to use the gifts He entrusts to you or to bury them? If you are afraid to risk them, what does that say about your trust in God, who provided them?*

3. *What do you have that is not a gift from God? What in your life can you take credit for as your own? What do you "own"?* (Answer: nothing is ours except our sin; everything else is a direct blessing or the result of a blessing from God)

Thinking it Through

What are things you can proactively do in your life to avoid the sin of sloth or laziness in your faith walk? What are the ways that you can grow in your zeal to build the Kingdom, daily? How does God insure you have access to such zeal and greater power to unleash the gifts He gives you?

Additional Verses:

Jeremiah 1:4-8
Luke 9:62
Ephesians 2:10
2 Corinthians 11:23-30
James 5:20

Closing Prayer

Have the teens each take a turn offering up one "thing" they can do, today, to eliminate or battle one of the sins of omission in their lives. Allow everyone to offer something before closing in a more formal prayer.

Have a teen lead a prayer for the Holy Spirit to come upon the group and unleash greater power and initiative to discern their vocations, live for God and work in His name.

INTERESTING FACTS ABOUT JEWISH CULTURE

As we mention in the *Interesting Facts about the Holy Land* section, knowledge about the geography and culture of the Bible makes all the stories, characters, and history come to life for you, the modern reader.

Below are some random facts that you might find interesting:

- Imagine a world without cars. In biblical times, traveling by foot meant you traveled no more than fifteen miles a day, while a donkey caravan moved about twenty miles a day. A camel, however, could go more than fifty or sixty miles a day.
- There are more than 300 references to trees in the Bible. Trees were essential for shelter, building, tools, and fuel.
- Clothing was made principally of sheep's wool or cheap linen. Other fabrics, such as fine linen and silk, were also used, but they were far too expensive for the average working class Jewish family.
- As a sign of mourning, men often shaved off their beards.
- Women's perfume was made of frankincense, aloe, spikenard, and/or myrrh.
- A new "day" began at dusk. So sunrise didn't mark the new beginning of a new day, rather sunset the night before did.
- Music played an important role in the life and worship of the Jews and early Christians. Instruments discussed in Scripture include the flute, harp, lyre, shofar, trumpet, cymbals, bells, and gongs.
- Beds were little more than mats, and they were often quite coarse. Blankets or coverings were often made of goat hair, and pillows were made from goatskin and stuffed with feathers or wool.
- The Romans revolutionized travel by creating pavements and stone roadways in place of the commonly-used dirt paths.
- The "Day of Atonement" (*Yom Kippur*) was a day of mourning that is still observed by Jews. Its beginnings can be traced back to the book of Leviticus.
- There was an amazing engineering achievement created by a group called the Jebusites. They lived long before Jesus (even before King David), but they built an underground tunnel system that brought fresh water into Jerusalem from a spring below. After tapping that stream, people within the city needed only to lower their buckets for fresh water and not leave the city.
- When people put on their sandals, they always put on the right before the left. They took their sandals off in that order, too.

LEADER'S NOTE

The New Testament was written within the culture of first-century Palestine, so it is essential for teens to understand some of the cultural idioms and practices of that period. If they do not understand something of the culture of the time, a significant portion of the biblical narrative will be lost on them. So take the time to point out and explain as many of these cultural issues as possible.

The list of bullet points on page 17 of the Student Workbook (above) explains some random facts regarding Mediterranean and early Jewish culture. There are several points that do not directly relate to the topics that are being discussed within the study, but they provide interesting conversation starters and can further whet your teens' appetites to learn more. Continually guide them back to their study Bibles, as well as to any footnotes and information you have from your own personal, ongoing biblical study. Do everything in your power to help your young people embrace the Mediterranean world as an actual place of real people who existed in "real time."

THE FAMILY TREE OF JESUS

It's important to know where you come from. It's even more important to know where you are going. The first eighteen verses of Matthew's gospel is what's called a **genealogy**, a study of "descent" tracing generation by generation up the family tree (from the roots).

Since Matthew is writing to Jews, he traces the bloodline of Jesus Christ all the way back to Abraham, the great patriarch and forefather of faith.

You might wonder what this has to do with you today or what purpose it could possibly serve to know the family tree of Jesus. You might even think, like most do, that it's really only important to know the New Testament. Nothing could be further from the truth. The better you understand the Old Testament and its characters, the more the New Testament comes to life. In turn, the more you read the New Testament, the more you'll discover the Old Testament, literally and figuratively, within its pages.

Don't just begin your experience of the gospel of Matthew with the eighteenth verse of chapter one. Take some time and read more about those in Jesus' family tree, the people listed below. I've even included book/chapter/verse for many of them, so you can see where their personal stories "began" in the Scriptures. It might surprise you to see and learn how much you have in common with Jesus. He wasn't born into a "perfect" family tree. Many of the ancestors in Jesus' line lived far less than saintly lives; that reality is truth and should give us great hope.

You know how the story "ends," with Jesus' ascension and the birth of the Church. Now, go back and see how it all began.

"The book of the genealogy of Jesus Christ, the son of David, the son of Abraham..." (Matthew 1:1)

MATTHEW 1:1-18

Abraham (Abram) – Gen. 17:5
Isaac – Gen. 17:19
Jacob - Gen. 25:26
Judah and his brothers - Gen. 29:35
Perez (by Tamar) - Gen. 38:29
Hezron - Gen. 46:9
Ram –1 Chron. 2:9
Amminadab – 1 Chron. 2:10
Nahshon - 1 Chron. 2:10-11
Salmon – Ruth 4:20-21
Boaz (by Rahab) – Ruth 2:1
Obed (by Ruth) – Ruth 4:17
Jesse – 1 Sam. 16:1
David the king – 1 Sam. 16:13
Solomon (by the wife of Uriah – Bathsheba) – 2 Sam. 12:24
Rehoboam – 1 Kgs. 11:43
Abijah – 1 Chron. 3:10
Asa – 1 Kgs. 15:8
Jehoshaphat – 1 Kgs. 15:24
Joram – 2 Kgs. 3:1
Uzziah – 2 Kgs. 15:13
Jotham – 2 Kgs. 15:17
Ahaz – 2 Kgs. 15:38
Hezekiah – 2 Kgs. 16:20
Manasseh – 2 Kgs. 21:1
Amos – 2 Chron. 32:20
Josiah – 2 Kgs. 21:24
Jechoniah (deportation to Babylon) – 1 Chron. 3:16, Esth. 2:6
She-alti-el – 1 Chron. 3:17
Zerubbabel – Ezra 3:2
Abiud, Eliakim, Azor, Zadok , Achim , Eliud, Eleazar , Matthan, Jacob – Matt. 1:13-16
Joseph the husband of Mary – Matt. 1:16
Jesus was born, who is called Christ – Matt. 1:21

"Now the birth of Jesus Christ took place in this way. When his mother Mary had been betrothed to Joseph, before they came together she was found to be with child of the Holy Spirit..." (Matthew 1:18)

LEADER'S NOTE

The "family tree" (or genealogy) of Jesus found on page 18 of the Student Workbook is obviously not the most exciting reading for your average, post-modern adolescent. It is not a topic most *adults* would read or study, either. This family tree, however, is vital to understanding Jesus' identity. Put simply, spending time Jesus' genealogy is not a waste of time. Whether or not it is successfully received by the teens depends (in large part) on how hard successful you are a leader in drawing out its relevance.

If time permits, have your teens discuss their own family trees. Have them see how far back they can trace their lineage. The most important thing that you can do is to take out the names of some of the biblical "family members" they do recognize, and spend a few moments on the chapters listed next to them. Help your young people to understand who these characters are and how their lives are similar. Even a broad stroke, cursory examination of the characters' lives will go a long way in helping them understand the imperfect family tree of Jesus; that comprehension will help them to more easily embrace the imperfections in their own family trees.

History of the Nativity "Set"

You may have a Nativity set beneath your Christmas tree or on a table inside your house. You almost certainly have one on display somewhere around your local Church. Many people don't realize that St. Francis of Assisi is credited with being the first person to "create a nativity scene", using live people and animals to bring the birth of Jesus "to life" in 1223. The coolest part of St. Francis' "living Nativity" was not the idea to do it.

Don't get me wrong, that was a creative thought, but it wasn't the most impressive insight.

What was most impressive is the fact that St. Francis used living people rather than paintings or statues in his "nativity scene." While statues, figurines and pictures are useful and effective, using humans and animals added a different, important dimension to the purpose of the nativity scene (or *crèche*, as it is known to many).

Statues, paintings and other works of art in Churches help us visualize and focus our minds in prayer. They're especially useful to those of us who have a difficult time concentrating. It's not like we worship the wood or paint, obviously; these forms and elements are just used as a tool to help us enter more deeply into prayer. [1]

As you look at the Nativity scene, whether in your home or in your parish, spend time contemplating each of the "characters" or "figures" that you see within it.

Focus on what each must have been thinking about or wondering about Jesus. Putting yourself in their shoes (well, sandals) is the first step into a deeper, richer prayer life.

- Consider what the **Blessed Virgin Mary** must have been thinking.
- Reflect on how humbled and filled with awe **St. Joseph** must have felt.
- Ponder how important this moment was in history, that God would send a host of **angels** to proclaim the event (like a proud Father would).
- Stop to reflect on what a bold statement it made inviting the **shepherds**, who were often thought of as the least popular and least desirable people in the community.
- Contemplate how far the **wise men** had traveled and what a significant statement they made not only with their gifts, but in their worship of the Christ.

Do you allow yourself to be a living, interactive participant in Jesus' story? Do you see yourself as part of the unfolding drama of salvation history? If not than you're probably not looking closely enough at the gospels. Don't stop with the Nativity, get back to **Matthew 1-2**, and encounter the source of St. Francis' inspiration.

Notes

[1] Mark Hart, *Ask the Bible Geek 2: More Answers to Questions from Catholic Teens* (Cincinnati: Servant Books, 2007), p. 55

Leader's Note

The nativity set is a great way to draw the past and the present together. It is also a great way to "bridge the gap" between cultural and ritualistic things we do as Catholics. Often teens view characters of Scripture as characters in a story. So spend some time connecting the dots for your teens between the rituals of our liturgies and in our homes and the "real people" of the Bible; the goal is to make the biblical figures relevant to their lives.

Discuss the creation and purpose of St. Francis' original nativity set (or crèche). Use this as a springboard to discuss how the lives of the great saints affect us today because of the things they did to bring forward the message of Christ in their time.

Ask for any other examples the teens can think of that are traditions in their home or parish, traditions such as the Jesse tree or Christmas lights. Have them lead discussions on how these rituals and practices bring more practical, tangible meaning to the Gospel.

Temptations vs. Trials

Written by God ... brought to you by the Bible Geek®

Begin with the Lord's Prayer (Our Father).

- What does the phrase "lead us not into temptation" mean to you?
- Do you believe that God leads you into and through trials?
- Do you believe that God leads you into temptations or are those from the devil?
- Do you think God allows you into situations that are "just too much" for you?

Read **1 Corinthians 10:13.**

What is this saying to us?

Read the following three passages, one at a time.

- Jesus in the desert – **Lk 4:1-13**
- Jesus in the garden – **Mt 26:36-46**
- Jesus on the Cross – **Lk 23:33-39**

Identify the likenesses and differences between temptation and trial.

Discuss and define each and where each one comes from.

Now, spend some time praying through the following verses.

Take time to journal about them. Underline verses that strike you. Write out questions you have as you go along.

What does the Bible say about temptation?

James 1:12-16, Mk 7:15, 21-23, 1 Tim 6:9-10, 2 Cor 2:11

What does the Bible say about trial?

James 1:2-4, Sirach 2:1, Jn 16:33

What does the devil try to accomplish with temptation?

Mt 13:19, 1 Cor 7:5, 1 John 5:19, 2 Thes 3:3

What does God accomplish through trials?

Rom 8:18, Heb 12:7, Ps 141:5

What we can accomplish through our responses?

Sirach 33:1, Sirach 51:12, 1 Pet 1:6-7

List some temptations and trials in your life:

____

____

____

____

Let the Spirit open your eyes to God's truth and His call in your life.

What is God showing you about these "trials"?

What comes from God?

What comes from your sin?

Look up one of the following verses and meditate on it each day for the following week:

Prov 1:10-11,15

Titus 2:11-12

Micah 6:8

Ps 32:8

Luke 22:28

Psalm 141:2-4

Rev. 3:8-11

Commit this to memory:

Hebrews 2:18=

Closing Prayer – Pray the Lord's Prayer (Our Father) again, slowly.

Leader's Note

The Our Father says "lead us not into temptation," and this is often a source of confusion for teens. Many see God as an absentee Father who is uninvolved in our lives on a daily basis. Others believe in a "prosperity Gospel"– i.e., if they do good things, God will bless them and protect them from suffering. So a Bible study that discusses the difference between temptations and trials–and how they relate to one another–is amazingly practical and necessary for teens. Utilizing this study will go a long way in helping teens make the proper distinction between what God positively wills and what He merely allows for a greater good (i.e., His permissive will).

Spend some time working through the Scripture verses on temptation and on trial found on page 20 of the Student Workbook. This will go a long way in helping teens understand that when bad things happen this isn't because God doesn't love them–and to see how God can make all things can work for the good. You might want to take some time thinking of some appropriate examples of temptations and trial to share that can more clearly delineate the difference between the two, bringing to light the differences between obstacles and an opportunities.

THE BEATITUDES OVERVIEW

The **Sermon on the Mount** is the "most famous sermon ever preached" according to most people. What's interesting, though, is that many people think that the Sermon on the Mount only includes the Beatitudes or that the Beatitudes are all about "being a nice person." If you read through **Matthew 5-7**, however, you'll soon see that the Sermon is far more than the Beatitudes and that it is not about "being nice."

That being said, the **Beatitudes** are challenging, beautiful and life-changing, if you let them really penetrate your heart. They call all of us men and women alike, to become more Godly, every day.

The Beatitudes might be the best known and least obeyed of anything Jesus ever said.

PRAY THEM AGAIN:

"Seeing the crowds, he went up on the mountain, and when he sat down his disciples came to him. And he opened his mouth and taught them, saying:

- Blessed are the poor in spirit, for theirs is the kingdom of heaven.
- Blessed are those who mourn, for they shall be comforted.
- Blessed are the meek, for they shall inherit the earth.
- Blessed are those who hunger and thirst for righteousness, for they shall be satisfied.
- Blessed are the merciful, for they shall obtain mercy.
- Blessed are the pure in heart, for they shall see God.
- Blessed are the peacemakers, for they shall be called sons of God.
- Blessed are those who are persecuted for righteousness' sake, for theirs is the kingdom of heaven.
- Blessed are you when men revile you and persecute you and utter all kinds of evil against you falsely on my account.

Rejoice and be glad, for your reward is great in heaven, for so men persecuted the prophets who were before you."

- Matthew 5:1-12

NOTES

LEADER'S NOTE

On the surface, the Beatitudes might seem like an easy topic to present to teens, but nothing could be further from the truth. Often, this is *not* the topic that teens will easily or willfully discuss because they don't really understand what they mean. Out of a fear of looking foolish, many may not participate in the discussion at all.

When talking about as deep a topic as the Beatitudes, the best thing is to do your homework ahead of time. Read the footnotes in your Bible, the *Catechism of the Catholic Church,* and reflections from the saints on this important part of the Gospel. In addition, be ready with practical examples of each of the beatitudes, showing how they can be lived out in a teen's daily life.

Don't treat this as an academic, "question-and-answer" time. The Beatitudes should not be presented this way or the teens may mistake them for yet another "laundry list" of things they need to do; they will miss that the Beatitudes are meant to form their heart and change their perspective. Encourage the group to read through them in silence and then slowly walk them more deeply into the very heart of Jesus Christ.

What Christ is saying here is deep and can get, simply put, a little confusing if we rush through it. Sometimes it helps to take it one line at a time to better "see" and "hear" what Jesus is teaching us. Consider the following ideas when praying the Beatitudes line by line:

- Put your trust in God - Mt 5:3
- Repent of your sins - Mt 5:4
- Learn gentleness - Mt 5:5
- Become righteous- Mt 5:6
- Show mercy - Mt 5:7
- Seek and grow in holiness - Mt 5:8
- Make peace - Mt 5:9
- Rejoice through persecution - Mt 5:10-12

Take time to journal about these and pray about them. Put simply, the **Beatitudes** should "be your attitude" toward life, your family and friends and anyone else God puts before you each day. It's simple, really ... it's just not easy.

NOTES

The Our Father: An Overview

You know the Our Father. You've probably recited it a thousand times.

But how many times have you really prayed it? How many times have you meditated slowly on each word and allowed the word to implant itself in your heart, to imbed itself in your soul?

The Our Father is the perfect prayer. It sums up everything we need to know about our relationship to God the Father and His relationship to us as His children. You could pray just this prayer every day for the rest of your life and never exhaust its richness or the depths of its truth.

Pray it again, slowly:

> Our Father who art in heaven, Hallowed be thy name. Thy kingdom come. Thy will be done, on earth as it is in heaven. Give us this day our daily bread; and forgive us our trespasses, As we forgive those who trespass against us; and lead us not into temptation, But deliver us from evil.
>
> – Matthew 6:9-13

Now, take it slowly, line by line and pray it, again.

As you go, read through some of the questions below, to help you enter into the prayer even more deeply...

Now, take it slowly, line by line and pray it, again.

After you've prayed it a few times slowly, move on to the journaling exercise that follows.

Journaling through the Our Father

Under each phrase below, take some time to journal and reflect. Pay attention to the words. Ask yourself, "Do I really believe this truth? Do I really live this truth?"

Underline or highlight or circle words below that really "stand out" to you within the prayer. Reflect upon why those words resonate more deeply with you.

Spend time journaling, writing about, the questions or thoughts that come to you as you pray through each phrase, one at a time.
Take time to identify areas of your life in which you really do live out the prayer and the areas in which you might struggle the most.

Work through the entire prayer before reading back through what you've journaled here. Once you've filled in this area, don't let that stop you. This is a useful journaling prayer exercise you can do anytime, any day. It's especially useful to journal when you feel too "tired" or "unfocused" to pray. You'll often be amazed at what comes out when you put the pen to the paper.

Let the Holy Spirit lead you into this form of prayer. There is no wrong response or reflection. Take some time now to pray the Our Father in this new way:

Leader's Note

Since the teens already know the Our Father, they may not be open to taking a closer look at it. They see the familiar words and gloss right over them, moving on to another topic that seems more interesting . But, truth be told, there is no more essential prayer they could ever study and pray than the Our Father.

Be sure to take the time to discuss this section with your teens. Walk them through the Our Father, intentionally and methodically. Journey through this prayer, line by line. The gift of time that you are allotting to this exercise will not be wasted.

This is the perfect prayer—and it is has been since the moment it first left our Savior's lips when he taught it to His apostles.

The Our Father: An Overview

Our Father,

Who art in Heaven,

Hallowed be thy Name;

Thy Kingdom come;

Thy Will be done

On earth as it is in Heaven.

Give us this day our daily Bread,

And forgive us our trespasses

As we forgive those who trespass against us.

And lead us not into temptation

But deliver us from evil.

Amen.

The Miracles in Matthew

Jesus once said, "Unless you people see signs and wonders, you will not believe" (John 4:48).

Modern-day followers of Jesus often fall into the same trap. Maybe you've prayed for God to "show you a miracle" so that you would believe. While God does promise that he hears our prayers and will give us what we need if we ask him in faith, we have to remember that what we want is not always what we need.

The miracles that Jesus performed weren't done in an effort to wow the crowds or to make people believe that he was God. His miracles always had a larger purpose than just a "cool trick" he pulled over nature or just alleviating someone's personal suffering. The miracles of Christ always pointed people back to His Father and to the Kingdom of God, not to building His reputation or popularity.

As the *Catechism* tells us, "Moved by so much suffering Christ not only allows himself to be touched by the sick, but He makes their miseries His own, 'He took our infirmities and bore our diseases.' But he did not heal all the sick. His healings were signs of the coming of the Kingdom of God. They announced a more radical healing: the victory over sin and death through His Passover" (*CCC* 1505).

It's important not to fall into the "trap" of trying to explain away the miracles of Christ through science or sociology. Such pursuits are inconsistent with Church teaching and with the very heart of God. Christ's miracles prove not only the power God has over sin and death, but a larger reality of God's willingness to heal you and work miracles in your life in accordance with His will.

Take some time to pray through the following miracles that Jesus performed. Pay attention to the who, the what, the when and where and how, but, as always, really ask yourself, "*Why* did Jesus do this? How does it point me back to the kingdom?"

	Matthew
Healing of the crowd in Galilee	4:23-25
Many healings	8:16-17
Healing of a leper	8:1-4
Healing of Centurion's servant	8:5-13
Healing of Peter's mother-in-law	8:14-15
Calming of the storm at sea	8:23-27
Healing of wild men at Gadara	8:28-34
Healing of the lame man (paralytic)	9:1-8
Healing of the woman with a hemorrhage	9:20-22
Raising of Jairus' daughter	9:23-26
Healing of two blind men	9:27-31
Healing of possessed man	9:32-34
Healing of man with withered hand	12:9-13
Feeding of the 5,000+ people	14:13-21
Walking on water (Sea of Galilee)	14:22-33
Healing of Gentile's daughter	15:21-28
Healing of the multitude	15:29-31
Feeding of 4,000+ people	15:32-39
Healing of an epileptic boy	17:14-21
Finding the money in the fish	17:24-27
Healing of the man with unclean spirit	1:21-27
Healing of the crowds in Judea	19:1-2
Healing of Bartimeaus (blind)	20:29-34
Healing of many in Jerusalem	21:14
Resurrection	28:1-10

Leader's Note

Some theologians today have tried to dismiss—or "reinterpret"—the miracles of Jesus in the name of science, enlightenment, or "reason." When dealing with a topic as fundamental to our Faith as Christ's miracles, it is crucial that you be firm and clear in what you teach your teens.

This is a great opportunity to explain and reaffirm the Church's position on the divinity of Christ and the historical character of His miracles. There is no room for ambiguity on this point. If Christ did not perform the miracles described in the gospels, then our entire exegetical process is suspect and the early Church is untrustworthy. Our Faith teaches, of course, that Jesus did in fact perform miracles, miracles that defied reason ... and with a good reason.

Pray through each account and select specific miracles you believe appeal most directly to your own teenagers. (Feel free to utilize *T3* DVD 4, segment 7 as a teaching aide to help drive the point home.)

THE PARABLES IN MATTHEW

The word "parable" comes from the Greek word *parabole* which means "a comparison." Jesus often communicated the truths of God and the coming kingdom of God through parables. As the *Catechism of the Catholic Church* teaches, "Through His [Jesus] parables he invites people to the feast of the kingdom, but he also asks for a radical choice: to gain the kingdom, one must give everything" (*CCC* 546).

Parables are particularly useful in modern biblical study because they are simple truths expressed in very practical, easy-to-understand ways, with visuals and concepts that even the most hardened heart can comprehend. Part of the modern difficulty in studying the parables, though, is that we often don't know too much about life in the Holy Land 2,000 years ago, and much needs to be explained. In addition, some parables are only understood over time and through faith. It is through the "eyes of faith" that disciples (John 20:29), both in biblical times and in the modern day, sometimes come to the deepest understanding of the love and person of Jesus Christ.

As you read and pray through these parables, be sure to take the time to read the footnotes in your Bible. Also, write out questions that you have as they arise and take the time to ask them to your parish priest, parent, youth minister, adult leader, or some other teacher of the faith. In addition, there are several other texts that can help you better understand the teachings and parables of Christ. It's just like anything else in your life, the harder you work at it, the better you'll be at it...it just takes time and practice.

	Matthew
What Jesus said about Parables	13:10-17, 34-35
Sower	13:3-9, 18-23
Wheat and tares	13:24-30, 36-43
Mustard Seed	13:31-32
Leaven	13:33
Treasure in the field	13:44
Pearl of great price	13:45-46
Net	13:47-50
Householder	13:52
Laborers in the vineyard	20:1-16
Two sons	21:28-32
Wicked husbandmen	21:33-36
Marriage of king's son	22:1-14
Fig tree	24:32-36
Ten Virgins	25:1-13
Talents	25:14-30
Sheep, goats	25:31-46

NOTES

LEADER'S NOTE

Encourage the teens to ask you any questions they might have after reading—and praying about—any of Jesus' parables listed on page 26 of the Student Workbook. This means more work for you as leader, but the effort is well worth it.

There are several good commentaries—some academic, others more "spiritual"—available on the parables of Jesus. Choose one to use for reference. You will find this useful in your personal study and ongoing prayer. If a teen asks a question or is looking for more insight and you are unsure of the answer, don't panic. Assure your group that you will investigate the issue a little further and will get back to them later. You do not need to know every answer to every question a young person may ask about the Bible. Rather, the important thing is to exemplify a well-informed and passionate hunger for God's word that will give your teens hope that the Gospel is something to be experienced and lived, not merely studied.

The Apostles

Are you bad with names?

Can you name the Seven Dwarfs? Happy, Grumpy, Sleepy, Sneezy, Bashful, Dopey, and Doc.

How about the six "main characters" of *High School Musical*? Troy, Gabriella, Sharpay, Ryan, Chad, and Taylor.

OK, now how about the names of the twelve apostles?

I conducted an informal interview of about fifty Christians over the past couple of weeks (Christians who are very active in their faith) and only four could name all twelve apostles. It's harder than it sounds. So, before you read anymore, grab a piece of scrap paper and a pencil and try it. I'll wait.

OK, how did you do?

St. Matthew gives us the names in **10:2-4** of his gospel, they are:

1. Simon (Peter)
2. Andrew
3. James (the Greater, brother of John)
4. John
5. Philip
6. Bartholomew (Nathanuel)
7. Thomas
8. Matthew (Levi)
9. James (the Lesser, son of Alphaeus)
10. Jude (Thaddeus)
11. Simon (the Zealot)
12. Judas (Iscariot)

I made up the following sentence (each word's first letter signifies a different apostle) to help me remember them:

"**SP**iritual **A**nd **J**oyful, **T**hey **P**roclaimed...**J**ust **B**y **J**oining **M**ary's **S**on **J**esus' **J**ourney."

In other words: Simon (Peter), Andrew, James, Thomas, Philip, John, Bartholomew, James, Matthew, Simon, Jude, Judas

So, is it absolutely essential that you memorize and know all of the twelve apostles' names? Well, probably not. But, then again, they were recorded for a reason and each one (except Judas) went on to live a passionate life, living and dying for their beliefs in Jesus. The word "apostle" is different than "disciple." *Apostle* means "one who is sent." The apostles were special, they were set apart and they fulfilled a special mission ... to go out and proclaim Christ in a world of people who did not know Him. They are our "older brothers" in the faith, our first bishops and our first priests. They, along with Mary and the saints and martyrs, are our role models in the faith. That's pretty impressive.

The way I look at it, it never hurts to grow deeper in knowledge and really know our faith. I mean if I can name the cast of *High School Musical* or the seven dwarfs, I should at least be able to name Jesus' twelve. And the better we know the Bible, the more we'll be able to offer people than just "memorized verses." Don't get me wrong, it's great to be able to quote verses at appropriate times, but the more we get to know the book's primary characters in addition to the words ... the better we get to know the Author who created and called them, and who created and calls us.

"Spiritual And Joyful, They Proclaimed...Just By Joining Mary's Son Jesus' Journey."

While the Bible doesn't record how most of the apostles died, traditions tell us the manner in which they were martyred. Traditions and legends vary, but here are some of the more "commonly held" explanations of the apostles' deaths:

Leader's Note

Learning about the apostles is more than learning about "facts" about the gospel or about the "supporting characters" in the story. In the apostles, we as modern disciples of Jesus will find virtues that we can relate to and by which we will be challenged.

Even those apostles we don't know have much information about in the pages of Sacred Scripture deserve our attention and prayerful contemplation. There is a reason that these particular twelve men were selected by Jesus. Each has some specific talent or skill that he Jesus would use to build up the Kingdom.

When we look at the lives of the apostles, we are presented with real life encounters that break through teenagers' cliques, personalities, doubts, and anxieties. The apostles offer us the a wide array of personality and character types to which any teenager can be drawn. Whether a teen is a natural leader or a little "sheepish," verbose, or silent, the better he knows the apostles, the better he will understand that Christ calls him now for a reason—just as He called the apostles.

THE APOSTLES

THE APOSTLES

1. Peter was crucified upside down
2. Andrew was crucified in Egypt
3. James was beheaded for preaching Christ in the temple
4. John died naturally
5. Phillip was hanged from column of the great temple
6. Nathaneal was skinned alive and crucified in double agony
7. Thomas was speared by an angry mob
8. Matthew's martyrdom is not certain, whether burned, stoned, or beheaded.
9. James Alphaeus was thrown off the roof of Herod's temple
10. Jude Thaddeus was crucified and shot to death with arrows
11. Simon the Zealot was sawed to pieces alive
12. Judas Iscariot hung himself

May these courageous martyrs pray for us now, and at the moment of our own death.

NOTES

Do you "see" what I "see"?

Have you ever noticed how often you hear about the "Pharisees" and "Sadducees" at Mass? Have you noticed how much trouble they got themselves into with Jesus? Have you ever stopped to find out just what made these groups so important and so controversial within Jesus' proclamation of the Kingdom?

Until a few years ago, I didn't really know the difference between the Pharisees and Sadducees, either. In fact, if we took a survey of Catholics, I think we would discover that most don't know the differences between these two groups, either. But let's see if we can give you enough quick information to put you in the minority who do know.

Pharisees and Sadducees were different Jewish "sects" before, during, and after the time of Jesus. (A *sect*, simply put, is a group of people with somewhat different or separate religious beliefs.)

Pharisees

The term *Pharisee* comes from a Hebrew word that means "separate." In the time of Jesus, they were the popular religious political party (see John 7:48). They came about a few centuries before Christ when the Greeks were forcing the Jews to abandon their religious practices. What started as a needed thing, however, over time became a bad thing.

What we need to understand about the Pharisees is that they were extremely legalistic and followed the Law of Moses in extremely exacting ways (see Matthew 9:14, 23:15p; Luke 18:12). They separated themselves from other Jews. While the intentions seemed pure and their creed was solid, their religion was more about form and function and not about surrender or humility. They were very self-righteous (Matthew 9; Luke 18) and Jesus laid into them (check out Matthew 12:9, 16:1-4).

The Pharisees "supplemented" the law by their own traditions, which took the law an unnecessary step or two further. They knew the law like the back of their hands, but not with the front of their hearts. That's why they had such a problem with Jesus when He came onto the scene. They believed in the coming of the Messiah, but denied that Jesus was the One—even though He fulfilled all of the Messianic prophecies that existed in the Scriptures (if their hearts would have been open enough to recognize this).

Sadducees

The Sadducees were also a Jewish sect. They probably began as a by-product of the Greek philosophy that was pervading the Mediterranean world prior to the time of Jesus. The first time we see them in the Gospel, they came out to challenge John the Baptist (Matthew 3). Jesus calls them hypocrites (Matthew 16). What we need to understand about the Sadducees (which makes them different from the Pharisees) is that they denied the doctrine of the resurrection, denied the existence of angels or spirits, and denied the obligation to follow oral traditions (beyond what was written down).

Many of them had a deep-seated hatred for Jesus, and they—along with the Pharisees—played a huge part in His condemnation. They hated the apostles, too, and tried to get them not to preach the resurrection (Acts 2, 4). After the destruction of Jerusalem in about A.D. 70, we don't hear much more about the Sadducees.

Scribes

The primary function of a scribe was to write stuff down, but to think of them solely as a sort of "secretary" would sell them short. Scribes were very important people in the Old Testament, writing and issuing decrees in the name of the king. They were very active in all affairs of state, probably given their ability to write and their more formalized educations.

Leader's Note

The Pharisees and the Sadducees are mentioned often throughout the gospels, and none more predominantly than in the gospel of St. Matthew. But, realistically, how much does the average teen *really* know about these groups?

On the surface, the Pharisees and Sadducees might not seem very interesting to a teen or even to most adults. The reality, however, is that a basic understanding of these groups of people immediately changes one's appreciation of the drama of the Gospel.

This is one of those moments when the teens will discern what is or is not important, mainly by your own attitude, tone and sense of urgency as you discuss this topic. Intrigue, excitement and interest are contagious. If there is urgency in you, they can see it and will respond. By extension, if you seem uninterested and seem as though this is just a mandatory "must know" to check off as they move through *Thy Kingdom Come*, they are going to check out.

When the Jews were taken into captivity in Babylon, the scribes took on a slightly different function—that of transcribing and promoting the law of Moses and insuring it was taught to the next generation of Jews. Ezra and Baruch are two of the most famous scribes in the Old Testament. They were devoted to the handing on and copying of the law to those who needed it badly. Most of the scribes were Pharisees. Even some who were Pharisees, though, were not hostile toward Christ or the apostles.

One more term you will hear when discussing and studying this cultural framework is *Sanhedrin.*

Sanhedrin

The term comes from a Greek word that means a "sitting together" or a "council." We see them in Matthew 5, Mark 15, and Matthew 26. Basically, the Sanhedrin was a council of seventy-one "elders" with the high priest sitting as a sort of "president." In the year of Jesus' crucifixion, the high priest was named Caiphas.

The Sanhedrin was made up of chief priests (twenty-four or so), scribes, and elders. They were the high court, if you will, and were the judicial and administrative voice for all Jewish matters religious and political. Their jurisdiction didn't just cover the Jews in Jerusalem, either, but Jews outside of Palestine as well.

There was a power struggle between the Sanhedrin, King Herod, and Rome which went on for years. It was the Sanhedrin that "tried" Christ before turning Him over to Pilate. It was the Sanhedrin that charged Peter and John (Acts 4, 5) with heresy, charged Stephen with heresy (Acts 6) and Paul for violations of the temple law (Acts 22-23). You can think of the Sanhedrin more like a Supreme Court made up of Democrats and Republicans. Different political agendas, upbringings, levels of education, and philosophies were all came together with one common purpose—to rule over the Jewish population.

To sum up

Basically, the Pharisees thought they knew better than everyone else. The Sadducees thought they were higher minded than everyone else. The scribes were better educated and (many) believed they were superior to others. The Sanhedrin wielded a lot of power and thought themselves "untouchable" by the token king Herod and annoying government of Rome. And then there was Jesus ... not sweatin' any of them. He knew who had (and has) the power.

Incidentally, if you want to read a great scene that depicts the differences and politics associated with the Pharisees and Sadducees, check out Acts 23:1-11. Here, you will see just how ingenious St. Paul was. He knew that the Sadducees didn't believe in the resurrection but that the Pharisees did. Spend some time reading the passage; read the footnotes as well. St. Paul certainly liked to "stir the pot."

Basically, the differences between the Pharisees, Sadducees, scribes, etc., are "small," but they are very important to gain a better understanding of the culture of the time and *why Jesus did what He did and said what He said.* Don't "read over" them and think that details such as these are irrelevant. They *are* relevant, and they teach us a lot about what Jesus had to deal with at the time. They teach us, too, a lot about the difference between following the law and living the law, following God and loving God.

Keep reading!

Notes

Leader's Note (Cont.)

As you discuss this topic try and set the stage. Explain how some of the Pharisees and Sadducees acted as Jesus' nemeses. Set a scene of debate. Underscore the tension by explaining what they thought of themselves. Help your young people understand just how much Jesus was up against, just how outnumbered He was in this way.

Possibly the best way to bring this to life is to draw on how both John the Baptist and Christ referred to them as hypocrites. Every teenager loathes hypocrites. No one wants to be considered one and most are willing to label hypocrisy in others. What is more interesting is that in moments of true authenticity and honesty, most teenagers are able to think of things they find hypocritical in their own life. Utilizing this point of contention as the foundation of discussion will go a long way in gaining their interest

APOLOGETICS SECTION

It's popular for Catholics today to be questioned about their faith and challenged on Church teachings. You might, for instance, have friends ask you, "Where is that in the Bible?" If you don't know the Bible very well, those types of questions can leave you feeling everything from confused to embarrassed. What you have to remember, though, is that you have 2,000 years of living tradition behind you, and even when your legs are "shaking" on the foundation of our Church the foundation of the Church is not shaking underneath you.

First of all, remember never to argue. You have nothing to argue about. Always try to focus on what we share in common with other faiths, first and foremost. When there's a spirit of respect, if someone wants to ask questions out of curiosity, or to learn more, then you can explain the Catholic faith.

Don't get in a defensive mode, you have no reason to get defensive, we are blessed to be part of the original Christian Church, founded and instituted by Christ, Himself. That's pretty cool, huh?

As for a more specific answer to that question of "Where does it say that in the Bible?", you might want to offer the following three verses, as a starting point:

"Therefore, brothers, stand firm and hold fast to the traditions that you were taught, either by an oral statement or by a letter of ours."

– 2 Thessalonians 2:15

In this verse, St. Paul is reminding the early Christians (who didn't have the gospels written down yet) that the **Traditions** that they were taught are important to follow and remember, both the traditions that had been written down, and the ones that were being modeled and passed along 'orally' by word of mouth.

Another great verse to further explain the importance of observing the teaching authority of the Church is the following:

"But if I should be delayed, you should know how to behave in the household of God, which is the church of the living God, the pillar and foundation of truth." – 1 Timothy 3:15

It reminds us that the **Church** is the foundation of truth. This is not to say that the Scriptures don't contain truth, they do (very obviously), and the Church plays an important role in interpreting the scriptures in the way that they are meant to be interpreted.

"All scripture is inspired by God and **is useful** for teaching, for refutation, for correction, and for training in righteousness." **– 2 Timothy 3:16**

This is another great verse. Notice that it say that the scriptures are useful, but not that they are the only source of training or correction.

There are literally dozens of books and countless websites that examine each of the most debated tenets of the Catholic faith. I'd encourage you to spend some time in your local Catholic bookstore and see which ones would be most helpful for you, specifically. In addition, you can always check out www.biblegeek.com. I've answered well over 200 of the most commonly asked questions regarding Scripture and the Catholic faith.

I wanted to take a minute, though, and give you a sort of "quick reference" guide to which Scriptures you can use, to explain in greater Scriptural detail, what we believe as Roman Catholics.

So, here's a list of ten Catholic teachings you'll probably be questioned most about and some of the verses it will help you to know:

1. The Blessed Virgin Mary – Her perpetual Virginity and Her place of honor
    - Lk 1:28
    - Lk 1:30, 34
    - Lk 1:42
    - Jn 19:26
    - Gn 3:15
2. The Papacy – where is that in the Bible?
    - Mt 16:18-19
    - Lk 22:32
    - Jn 20:23, 21:17
    - Acts 1:13-26
    - Acts 8:21
    - Acts 15:7, 28
    - 1 Tim 3:1, 8
    - 1 Tim 5:17

31

www.GreatAdventureOnline.com

LEADER'S NOTE

Many Catholics today use Scripture primarily for apologetics purposes. True, biblical apologetics is absolutely useful and worthwhile. But if we do not know the author of the Scriptures, we could use Scripture as a sword to divide. We would be more guilty than Peter when he unsheathed his sword in the Garden of Gethsemene.

Christ told Peter to put the sword back in its sheath. God wants us to know the Scriptures like the front of our heart rather than like the back of our hand. Verses listed in this section are not intended to further divide but to foster unity.

Sharing the truth should be always done in a fruitful and positive manner. As Catholics, we have nothing to defend, only to explain. The Church gave us the Bible. We should be honored and humbled to share the deepest revelation of truths entrusted to our Church and to share the Word in a way that fosters unity and depth. This will serve as a solid foundation for greater discussion with believers of any denomination and even non-believers.

APOLOGETICS SECTION

3. The Bible and Tradition (why the "Bible alone" is anti-Scriptural)
   - Mk 13:31
   - Mk 16:15
   - Jn 21:25
   - Rom 10:17
   - 1 Cor 11:2
   - 2 Thess 2:15, 3:6
   - 2 Tim 1:13, 2:2
   - 2 Pet 1:20
4. Faith and Works - (not by faith alone)
   - Mt 19:16-17
   - Jn 14:15
   - Rom 2:5-8
   - 1 Cor 13:2
   - Gal 5:6
   - Eph 2:8-10
   - Col 3:24-25
   - Jam 2:24-26
   - Rev 20:12-13
5. Eucharist – it's Scriptural
   - Mt 26:26
   - Jn 1:29
   - Jn 6:35-71
   - 1 Cor 2:14-3:4
   - 1 Cor 5:7, 10:16
   - 1 Cor 11:23-29
   - Ex 12:8, 46
6. Purgatory – it's Scriptural, too
   - Mt 5:26, 48
   - Mt 12:32-36
   - 1 Cor 3:15
   - 1 Cor 15:29-30
   - 2 Tim 1:16-18
   - Jas 3:2
   - 1 Pet 3:18-20, 4:6
   - 1 Jn 5:16-17
   - Rev 21-27
   - 2 Macc 12:44-46
7. Mary and the Saints – why it's okay to ask them to pray for us
   - Lk 16:19-30
   - Rom 8:35-39, 15:30
   - 1 Cor 12:12-27
   - Eph 6:18-19
   - 1 Thess 1:5-8
   - 1 Tim 2:1-7
   - Heb 12:1, 13:7
   - 1 Jn 3:2
   - Gal 6:10
8. Reconciliation – why we go to a priest
   - Mt 9:2-8
   - Mt 18:18
   - Jn 20:22-23
   - 2 Cor 5:17-20
   - Jas 5:13-16
   - 1 Jn 5:16

9 Salvation (why "once saved, always saved" isn't Biblical)
   - Mt 7:21, 10:22
   - Rom 8:24, 11:22
   - 1 Cor 9:27, 10:11-12
   - Gal 5:4
   - Eph 2:5,8
   - Phil 2:12
   - 2 Tim 1:9, 2:11-13
   - Heb 10:26-27
   - 1 Pet 1:9

10. The Priesthood – celibacy and why we call them "father"
   - Mt 19:19
   - Lk 14:26
   - Acts 7:2
   - Acts 21:40, 22:1
   - Rom 4:16-17
   - 1 Cor 4:14-15
   - 1 Thess 2:11
   - Heb 12:7-9
   - 1 Jn 2:13-14

LEADER'S NOTE (CONT.)

Be sure to emphasize that before the teens enter into an apologetically-based conversation with anyone, that an air of affirmation, respect, and prayerfulness are essential before discussing any hint of doctrine. Emphasize that Sacred Scripture and Sacred Tradition go hand-in-hand. Remind them of the unique gift of the Catholic Church, the guardian of truth, and the beauty of the Magisterium. all made possible through the inspiration and protection of the Holy Spirit. Don't be afraid to point to Vatican II's document *Dei Verbum* or the wealth of resources our Church has given regarding the importance of rooting our faith in the Word.

PERSONAL BIBLE STUDY ON THE PAPACY

We are so fortunate as Catholics that Christ instituted His Church here on Earth.

Before going on, read that phrase again because to some people it makes no sense. The truth is, however, that Christ *did* institute a Church, a foundation, through which and by which the Holy Spirit guides and leads us deeper into God's Divine Revelation.

"But," one might ask, "*why* would Jesus entrust His Church to humans ... to sinners"?

It's not like Jesus didn't know that people were going to sin. As God, He knew. The beauty of the Church, however, is that it stands as a guardian and interpreter of the Gospel of Christ, standing as a *pillar of truth* (see 1 Timothy 3:15).

Even when people within the Church sin (including any leaders) that **does not** render God's laws any less valid or true.

As we discussed in Session Five of the DVDs, the most common verse used to explain when Christ set Simon (Peter) above the other apostles in a leadership role is:

> And so I say to you (Simon), you are Peter, and upon this rock I will build my church, and the gates of the netherworld shall not prevail against it. I will give you the keys to the kingdom of heaven. Whatever you bind on earth shall be bound in heaven; and whatever you loose on earth shall be loosed in heaven (Matthew 16:18-19).

Notice all that Jesus does here.

1. Jesus changes Simon's name to Peter.
2. Jesus tells Peter that He is going to build His Church upon him.
3. Jesus promises that "the netherworld" will not prevail against the Church.
4. Jesus gives Peter "the keys."
5. Jesus gives Peter the power "to bind" and "to loose

Let's deal with each one briefly, in terms we can understand:

1. **Jesus changes Simon's name to Peter.**
   If you've been through *T3: The Teen Timeline*, recall the others whose names were changed by God. Remember—when He changes your name He changes your essence.

2. **Jesus tells Peter that He is going to build His Church upon him.**
   That's a straightforward enough thing that Jesus says, huh? Some people believe that the first time Jesus says "rock" that He is referring to Peter, and the second time He says it, that He's referring to Himself. A flawed interpretation for several reasons—specifically because of the proper Greek translation. The majority of biblical scholars all agree that Christ is referring to Peter in both instances.

3. **Jesus promises that "the netherworld" will not prevail against the Church.**
   OK, so *what* will evil never prevail against? Answer: the Church. People may try to point to scandals as some sort of proof that Christ was talking about Himself as the Church, not a Church on earth. That's simply not true. Battles may be lost, but not the war. The Church will always prevail; Christ promises us that.

4. **Jesus gives Peter "the keys."**
   The person with the keys is in the driver's seat (sometimes, literally) and nothing has changed in two thousand years. The keys not only let people in, they lock people out. The keys signify power.

   Also, think about what it says in **Luke 10:16**,

   > Whoever listens to you listens to me. Whoever rejects you rejects me. And whoever rejects me rejects the one who sent me.

LEADER'S NOTE

Most teens will not do a personal Bible study without much prompting and encouragement. Today, with the widespread use and ease of the Internet, it is important to affirm the validity of going back to the actual sources when discussing topics of such importance as the papacy and authority in the Church.

There are countless websites and resources filled with misinformation, exaggeration, lies, and half-truths, all designed to weaken the influence of the papacy and the authority of the Church. Such websites are very dangerous to Catholic young people—and all of them are only a mouse click away.

Taking the time to work through the Bible, showing some of the instances that demonstrate the primacy of Peter and institution of the papacy is invaluable. No website and no sociopolitical discussion regarding the papacy will be as powerful as having a teen read God's own words on the subject. This goes a long way toward addressing whatever concerns and questions that they might have about the institution of the papacy and will shed light on the God-given role of Peter and His successors as Vicar of Christ.

The one driving is the one who steers where the car is going. The other passengers can object (reject), but weren't given the keys, and, thus, can't steer. None of the other apostles get the keys, nor do any of the other New Testament figures. Think about it.

5. **Jesus gives Peter the power "to bind" and "to loose."**
   What does this mean? It refers to the sacramental power in the sacrament of reconciliation. Ask yourself, how would Peter, the apostles, or any priest know which sins "to bind" or "to loose," if they had not heard them, first.

   And Jesus is very clear, they have authority on earth that counts in heaven. I encourage you to read again the verses from Matthew 16 mentioned above before continuing.

Some other interesting biblical facts that are indisputable would include the following verses. Take the time to read through each verse and answer the questions below.

Matthew 10:2-4, Mark 3:16-19, Luke 6:12-19, Acts 1:13
Whose name appears first in each list?

Mark 8:29, John 6:68-69, and **Acts 2:14-41**
Who becomes the leader and "spokesman" for the apostles?

Luke 22:31-32
Who is the only apostle that Jesus personally prays for?

Luke 24:34, 1 Corinthians 15:5
Who did the resurrected Christ appear to first (out of the apostles)?

Mark 16:7
Who was singled out by the angels following the resurrection?

John 21:15-17
Who does Christ empower (as shepherd) to feed the sheep?

Acts 1:15-26
Who oversees the election of Judas' successor?

Acts 3:1-10
Who is the first apostle to work a miracle in Christ's name following Pentecost?

Acts 10:9-49
Who receives a special revelation from God regarding the Gentiles' place in the Church?

Galatians 1:18
Who does even St. Paul submit to?

You get the idea.

May God bless our Holy Father and all of our bishops, that they might continue to lead the flock with humility, boldness, wisdom and abandonment to God's will.

Pray **Matthew 16:16-20**, again, to close in prayer.

NOTES

Scripture in the Mass

There is no Sunday service of any Christian denomination or assembly that has more Scripture than the Catholic Mass. Our Liturgy has more Scripture than any other Christian service; that is a fact.

If this surprises you, it might just be that you haven't seen "where" so many of our commonly uttered prayers at Mass hail from.

See how many of these verses taken directly from Scripture you recognize hearing on a weekly basis:

- In the name of the Father and the Son and the Holy Spirit. –Matthew 28:19
- The Lord be with you. –Ruth 2:4
- Amen. –1 Chronicles 16:36
- Lord have mercy. –Tobit 8:4
- Christ have mercy. –1 Timothy 1:2
- Glory to God in the highest. –Luke 2:14
- Lord, I am not worthy to receive you. –Matthew 8:8
- Blessed be God forever. –Psalm 68:36
- May the Lord accept the sacrifice at your hands. –Psalm 50:23
- Holy, holy, holy Lord, God of power and might. –Isaiah 6:3
- Let us proclaim the mystery of our faith. –1 Timothy 3:16
- Lord, you are holy indeed, the fountain of all holiness. –2 Maccabees 14:36
- Take this and eat it, this is my body. –Matthew 26:26
- This is my blood of the covenant, which is poured out for many for the forgiveness of sins. –Matthew 26:28
- From age to age, you gathered your people to yourself. –Psalm 113:3
- Through Him, with Him, in Him. –Romans 11:36
- Go in peace to love and serve the Lord. –Luke 7:50; 2 Chronicles 35:5
- The grace of the Lord Jesus Christ, the love of God and the fellowship of the Holy Spirit be with all of you. –2 Corinthians 13:13

Remember, the Holy Mass is a contact sport, not a spectator sport. Pay attention to the prayers being offered and the words being spoken. Active listening is part of the "full, conscious, active participation" that the Church expects of you.

And if you want five ideas of how to "get more out of your Mass experience," here's my top five (in no particular order):

1. Be in a state of grace. If you need to get to confession, then be sure to go soon. Don't give the devil room to work and don't deprive yourself of the Eucharist.
2. Read through and pray the readings ahead of time. The Sunday readings are available in the Study Kit for T3, are always available online and probably listed in the bulletin at your Church. (In addition, check out the "Audio" section at www.biblegeek.com to listen to a free weekly podcast I offer, designed to help you navigate your way through the Sunday Mass readings!)
3. Sit where you can really enter into the Mass. If that means sitting closer, than sit closer ...don't be a pew warmer in the back of the Church. Sit as close to the "action" as you can. In addition, if you can't sit next to that one sibling or a certain friend at Mass without talking to them, than sit away from them. There will be plenty of time to fool around after Mass.

Leader's Note

Many Catholics are unaware of the actual amount of Scripture that is woven throughout the Mass. Even fewer are aware of the *context* of the Bible within the Liturgy. Only when a young person understands the context of words such as "Lord I am not worthy to receive you but only say the word and I shall be healed"–from Matthew, chapter eight–do they take on their proper meaning.

Don't just read through the different prayers given on page 35 of the Student Workbook. Instead take the time to remind them of all the Scripture they may know and not even realize. How many times have they said or heard one of these prayers and not known that it came directly from the Bible?

Possibly start the phrase, "Lord you are Holy indeed, you are..." and see if they can finish it with "...the fountain of all holiness." Start the phrase, "This is the blood of my covenant..." or with "May the grace of our Lord Jesus Christ, the love of God..." and let them finish either/both. Giving them lost little moments and letting them draw upon what they experience through Traditions will show them how much they actually do know about Scripture.

SCRIPTURE IN THE MASS

4. Be sure that you are tithing. The collection basket isn't just for adults–it's for everyone in the community. If you have a job or an allowance–basically if you have any income at all–you should be giving ten percent back to the Church (the ten percent is in the Bible; check out Genesis 14:18-20) and pray on 1 Peter 4:10. You are part of the community and you have a responsibility to support it. You are not the Church of "tomorrow," you are the Church of right now.

5. Dress for success. Mass is an encounter of the living God unlike any other. The liturgy is special, more special than anything else you do in the course of the day or week. Why do we allow ourselves to get "dressed up" to go on a date or to a dance, but not give a second thought to our appearance for Mass? Jesus is the VIP, and you're on his guest list...dress appropriately.

NOTES

PRAYING THE ROSARY

THE ROSARY

The Rosary is the most famous and most popular chaplet that we have as Catholics. A chaplet is a prayer devotion that commonly utilizes beads, it comes from a French word for "wreath" or "crown." While the structure and devotion of the rosary has its roots with the "desert fathers," it is **St. Dominic** who is historically credited with giving the structured gift of the Rosary to the greater Church.

In the Rosary we meditate on the life of Christ, gazing upon Him through the lens and window of Mary's soul. Since she is our Blessed Mother, gifted to us from His Cross **(John 19:27)**, it makes perfect sense that we would seek to look upon Christ in such an intimate and sinless way, as She does. The Rosary draws us into more perfect discipleship, and focuses our prayer on the Trinity.

This a prayer on a group of beads developed as a way to teach the life of Christ and Mary to those who were not able to read. It was also developed to assist those who were not clergy in praying the Liturgy of the Hours, the prayer of the Church. In the prayer we take our intentions to Mary and show our honor and respect for her as the greatest of all the saints and an example to us all.

The Rosary is divided into four sets of mysteries: Joyful, Luminous, Sorrowful, and Glorious. It is intended that, as we pray each "mystery," we meditate on the meaning of the event in the life of Christ and Mary and how we can apply this in our own lives.

Each Mystery has five decades and each decade is prayed in the following order: Our Father, Hail Mary, and the Glory Be. There are other prayers that are added onto the beginning and end of the Rosary, such as the Apostles' Creed and the Hail, Holy Queen. The prayer order for the Rosary is below along with indications of specific beads:

Joyful

1. The Annunciation
2. The Visitation
3. The Nativity of Jesus
4. The Presentation of Jesus
5. The Finding of Jesus

Luminous

1. The Baptism of Jesus
2. The Miracle of Cana
3. The Proclamation of the Kingdom
4. The Transfiguration
5. The Institution of the Eucharist

Sorrowful

1. The Agony in the Garden
2. The Scourging at the Pillar
3. The Crowning with Thorns
4. The Carrying of the Cross
5. The Crucifixion

Glorious

1. The Resurrection
2. The Ascension of Jesus
3. The Descent of the Holy Spirit
4. The Assumption of Mary
5. The Coronation of Mary

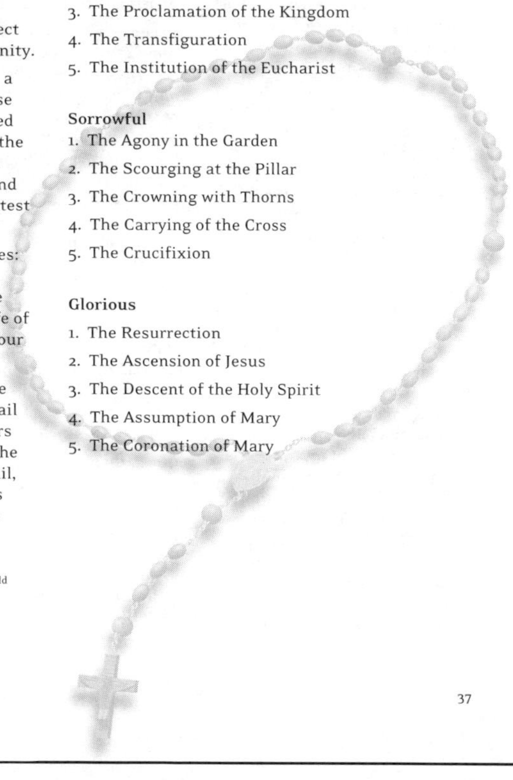

LEADER'S NOTE

The temptation is often to talk about a prayer rather than actually praying. Think about that for a minute. Is that what Christ is calling you to as a leader, to *talk* about prayer or to teach His little ones to pray?

Further, how much sense does it make for leaders to encourage teens to pray the Rosary if they themselves do not take advantage of this timeless, grace-filled devotion?

The Rosary is one of those rich and powerful devotions of our Faith, but if we don't look at the mysteries through the lens of Scripture it can easily become just a bunch of words being recited and repeated.

Take the time to pray the Rosary with your group—maybe while reading a few lines of Scripture for each mystery. This will enrich the prayer and doing so is also going to help your teenagers focus. We cannot separate the Rosary from Scriptures; they go hand in hand.

PRAYING THE ROSARY

HOW TO PRAY THE ROSARY

Sign of the Cross
Apostles Creed

Our Father - 1st Bead
3 Hail Marys - 3 beads
Glory Be

1st Mystery:
Our Father - single bead
10 Hail Mary - 10 beads
Glory Be

2nd Mystery:
Our Father - single bead
10 Hail Mary - 10 beads
Glory Be

3rd Mystery:
Our Father - single bead
10 Hail Mary - 10 beads
Glory Be

4th Mystery:
Our Father - single bead
10 Hail Mary - 10 beads
Glory Be

5th Mystery:
Our Father - single bead
10 Hail Mary - 10 beads
Glory Be

Hail, Holy Queen

It might be difficult for you to pray the rosary, because of the repetition of the prayers. I'll be honest with you, even though I pray it daily, it can still be tough for me sometimes. Repetition can have a soothing effect. The rhythm can be both a good thing and a bad thing (if you're like me). I have to work very hard to stay focused. Kneeling helps. That being said, it is a great gift. All prayer is directed to the Father, through Jesus Christ.

The Rosary is directed to Christ, guided by His mother. We should be thankful for the guided, Scriptural prayers (the Our Father, Hail Mary, Glory Be), always. They help us pray. At times they are all I can verbalize, when I'm too tired, distracted or too much in pain to muster anything else, of my own. And **remember** that we must always keep in mind Jesus' warning not to let our prayers become repetitious babbling or empty phrases (Matthew 6:7). Sometimes it helps to recite the prayers more slowly, to insure we are praying and not just saying the prayers.

PRAYERS

Apostles' Creed

I believe in God, the Father Almighty, Creator of heaven and earth and in Jesus Christ, His only Son, our Lord; Who was conceived by the Holy Spirit, born of the Virgin Mary, suffered under Pontius Pilate, was crucified, died, and was buried, He descended into hell; the third day He arose again from the dead; He ascended into Heaven, and sits at the right hand of God, the Father Almighty, from there He shall come to judge the living and the dead. I believe in the Holy Spirit, the Holy Catholic Church, the communion of saints, the forgiveness of sins, the resurrection of the body, and life everlasting. Amen.

Our Father

Our Father, who art in Heaven, hallowed be Thy name; Thy Kingdom come, Thy will be done on earth as it is in Heaven. Give us this day our daily bread; and forgive us our trespasses as we forgive those who trespass against us; and lead us not into temptation, but deliver us from evil. Amen.

Hail Mary

Hail Mary, full of grace, the Lord is with thee, blessed art thou amongst women and blessed is the fruit of thy womb, Jesus. Holy Mary Mother of God, pray for us sinners now and at the hour of our death. Amen.

The Doxology (Glory Be)

All Glory be to the Father, the Son and the Holy Spirit, as it was in the beginning, is now and ever shall be, a world without end. Amen.

Salve Regina (Hail Holy Queen)

Hail Holy Queen, Mother of Mercy, our life our sweetness and our hope. To thee do we cry, poor banished children of Eve; To thee do we send up our sighs, mourning and weeping in this valley of tears. Turn then, most gracious advocate, thine eyes of mercy toward us and after this our exile show unto us the blessed fruit of thy womb, Jesus. O clement, O loving, O sweet Virgin Mary!

LEADER'S NOTE (CONT.)

Anything you can do to continue to guide them back to tangible and relevant images of Scripture and to "connect the dots" between random prayers and living prayers is welcome—and will help them make the Rosary an active part of their faith lives.

AN OVERVIEW OF THE GOSPELS

All the books in the Bible are inspired by God and are free from error. That being said, among all of the Bible's seventy-three books, the four gospels are unique and supremely important.

In the gospels, we are not only given prophecies about the Messiah; we receive the Messiah Himself in flesh and blood. We encounter God in a entirely new way, and everything that we read about in the Law and the Prophets is now fulfilled.

Put simply, Jesus is the One that all have been waiting for, the One to whom we are called and invited to offer our lives. It is with the Gospel as your foundation that you will come to know the love of God and learn how to share that love with a world desperately in need of it. Everything you yearn to know, everything you wonder about God, every fear and every hope and every pain and every joy collide and find meaning within the Gospel of Jesus Christ. John Paul II put it this way: "It is Jesus that you seek when you dream of happiness; he is waiting for you when nothing else you find satisfies you...it is Jesus who stirs in you the desire to do something great with your lives."

The same Holy Spirit who inspired these words from John Paul II, moved through the pens of the four gospel writers, Matthew, Mark, Luke, and John. The Christ you encounter on the pages of their gospels is not a "nice Jesus," here to make everyone happy. Far from it. No, when you encounter Jesus in the gospels you see four portraits being painted of God, who became man in Christ Jesus.

Use these brief outlines to help you better understand the differences, but also the likenesses, in the Gospel portraits. Go back to the gospels repeatedly and you will notice something amazing. While the words and the truths don't change over time, they will change you over time, and over time you will hunger for them like you do regular food and spiritual food (Eucharist).

"It is written, 'Man shall not live by bread alone, but by every word that proceeds from the mouth of God."
- Matthew 4:4

NOTES

LEADER'S NOTE

How detailed the background you will offer your teens about each gospel will depend on the size, type, and age level of your group. That being said, this section in the Student Workbook is designed to give a "new reader" of the Bible enough footing to begin climbing.

There are several options you may want to consider as you present the gospels to your teens: 1) Explain how the three synoptic gospels differ from that of John; 2) Take a more critical look at the "historical" Jesus or the sayings of Jesus that are consistent across all four gospels; or 3) Discuss the official canon of Scripture and the non-canonical gospel texts that keeping resurfacing in conspiracy theories and popular movies (e.g., *The Da Vinci Code*).

One question will likely come up: "How can we trust the gospels when they differ on certain facts?" This presents a great opportunity to show the teens that such apparent discrepancies actually make the Scriptures even more believable. If they were too much alike, on every minute detail, there would be an even greater case that the Bible is not trustworthy.

AN OVERVIEW OF THE GOSPELS

Matthew

Author background

One of the original twelve apostles, Matthew (also called "Levi") was a tax collector working at a customs post when Christ invited him to follow (Mark 2:14).

Key themes for understanding Matthew's gospel:

- Jesus was the Messiah they had been waiting for
- Jesus did not come to abolish the law of Moses but to fulfill it (Matthew 5:17)
- Jesus came to begin His kingdom, one we are invited to enter by grace
- Jesus institutes a Church on earth to teach His truth and administer His sacraments

The central theme is that Christ the Messiah and King came to establish a Church.

Mark

Author background

We know very little about the author of this Gospel writer except that his name was probably birth name was John Mark (John is his Jewish name, Mark is his Roman name) and that he was a traveling companion of both Peter and Paul (2 Timothy 4:11, Colossians 4:10).

Key themes for understanding Mark's gospel:

- Jesus was powerful because He was a servant, not a conqueror
- Jesus is our mediator to God, He provides us with authority to teach, preach
- It was written to reaffirm to folks the primacy of Jesus Christ within the early Church, as apostles and eyewitnesses began dying off

The central theme is on action and service more than teaching.

Luke

Author background

Luke was not a Jew but a Gentile convert to Christianity. We also know that he was a physician by profession and as such was quite methodical in his approach to writing both the Gospel and Acts of the Apostles. Finally, we know he was a traveling companion to Paul for at least a while (Philippians 1:24, 2 Timothy 4:11, Colossians 4:14).

Key themes for understanding Luke's gospel:

- Emphasizes Jesus' compassion for the poor, needy, sick, helpless
- Reveals God's glory, mercy and desire/willingness to heal
- Focuses on the power of the Holy Spirit, God's grace and our salvation
- Uplifts the dignity of all women, especially the Blessed Virgin Mary
- Emphasizes prayer and humility

The central theme is liberation and healing.

John

Author background

John is believed to be writer of the final gospel, as well as of the three letters which bear his name and the book of Revelation. He was the younger brother of James, sons of Zebedee, the fishing partners of Peter. He is also called the "beloved disciple" (John 13:23, 19:26) who was entrusted with Mary's care at the Cross. He was most likely the youngest of the apostles, and lived the longest of all the Twelve. The writing of the gospel has extraordinary detail that had to be from an eyewitness.

Key themes for understanding John's gospel:

- John wasn't writing "another biography" of Jesus to add to the others; he assumes readers are familiar with the other gospels
- He wants to show that Jesus of Nazareth is the Son of God
- Desires to explain to Christians how to root their religious beliefs and practice in Jesus (sacraments) and how, by doing so, that faith will lead to eternal life
- Explains why He came, who He is and what He did and how it related to the life of the early church followers

The central theme is the identity of Jesus and what that means to our faith.

NOTES

AN OVERVIEW OF THE GOSPELS

FIRST-CENTURY PALESTINE

LEADER'S NOTE

When dealing with geography, many get bored. It is easy to get overwhelmed by a map–especially if the places listed are a two-thousand years old. Geography, however, will be easier to make interesting to your teens if it is put into context. The map and locations are far more relevant when we understand the amount of distance that Christ traveled North to south.

When we put places and events together, events take on a new meaning and all these situations become more real. If you can find a way to project the map they have in their study guides that is ideal. If not, walk them through the map in their guides.

Pick five or six events in the gospel of Matthew and point them out on the map. The better teens understand geography of the Gospel, the better they will understand God's interaction with His people. Anything you can do to insert fun into such an activity (even it requires a blank map and some sort of "contest") is worth the time. The interactivity will help teens retain the information .

Interesting Facts About the Holy Land

When it comes to Biblical geography, you're probably no expert. It's not like learning about ancient cities from the Mediterranean world is part of your "everyday conversation". That being said, the stories contained within the pages of Sacred Scripture, specifically within the Gospels, happened in actual places not fictional locations. Often times knowing even a few facts about the geography or the culture (which we will discuss a little later in this study guide) can make a huge difference in your understanding of a situation, or in the lesson you draw from it.

Below are some "random" and interesting facts about the Holy Land. Read through them and spend some time looking over the included map in this guide. The better you get the "lay of the land" the more that the Lord, His Word and the words in *Thy Kingdom Come* will come to life in your life.

Did You Know?

- When Jesus was only 12 years old, he walked 64 miles from Nazareth to Jerusalem (Lk 2:42). That round trip of 128 miles is the equivalent of walking from San Diego to Los Angeles.
- The Dead Sea is the lowest point on the face of the earth and it is the saltiest body of water in the world.
- Jerusalem is mentioned more in the Bible than any other city. It was seen by many to be "heaven on earth". It was sacked and destroyed by Rome in 70 A.D.
- The magi (wise men) were probably from modern day Iran or Saudi Arabia.
- Mountains are very important within Scripture. It was on Mt. Sinai that God gave Moses the Ten Commandments. It was on Mt. Ararat that Noah's Ark was reported to have landed. It was on Mt. Carmel that Elijah defeated the false prophets of Baal. It was on Mt. Tabor that tradition tells us Jesus was transfigured before His select apostles (although some claim it was Mt. Hermon).
- The Jordan River is Israel's longest river and is the most important river mentioned in all of Scripture. In it, Jesus was baptized, the Israelite crossed on dry land (it parted), Elijah parted it with his cloak and Elisha healed Naaman. It empties into the Dead Sea.
- The surface of the land in Palestine is made up mostly of limestone and chalk.
- There is a biting and powerful wind that can come in from the south (called the *hamsin*) that can be felt all the way to (and up) the coast. Jesus even referred to this wind in Luke 12:55.
- The surface area of the Sea of Galilee is about 13 by 5 miles. The Sea of Galilee also goes by the Lake of Genneserat (Lk 5:1) and the Sea of Tiberias (Jn 6:1, 21:1).

Leader's Note

Random facts and useless knowledge are very intriguing and often amusing to the average teenager. Teenagers want to be "in the know." They want to know things others don't know, especially adults.

If you preface this discussion with something like "You will soon know more than ninety percent of Catholics," you will quickly gain their attention. Never underestimate the allure of things that seem to serve no purpose than that of "entertainment value." Sometimes these are just the discussion starter you need to get a teen to finally take interest.

In addition, these facts are going to help make the stories more real to your teens. Compare the climates of the Bible to your own regional climate. If you are in the south (and know about intense humidity) talk to them about the more humid regions; if you are in the southwest, talk about living in a desert. If you live in a rural area where your young people have a strong understanding of farming and agriculture draw on those references in appropriate areas. Anything and everything that you can do to make theses associations and help the young people make the associations will help them pick up the scriptures on their own (away from the group).

- The Galilean area of Palestine (where Jesus lived) averages he highest amount of annual rainfall in the entire region.

- Jericho is about 3700 feet lower than Jerusalem. So, when the man in the Parable of the Good Samaritan "went down from Jerusalem to Jericho (Luke 10:30), he *literally was* going down over a half mile in altitude between the two cities of Jerusalem (2500 above sea level) and Jericho (1275 below sea level). So, even though Jericho is "north(east)" of Jerusalem, the man would still have been heading "down".

- On a modern day map you'd see that Jesus traveled from Egypt to Lebanon to Syria to Jordan. He did a lot of walking!

- Because of the immense amounts of underground water, caves are abundant throughout Palestine. People used them for shelter, hiding, dwelling, staging attacks, burial grounds, restrooms, storage and herding their animals.

- The climate of the Holy Land very unpredictable. It's not uncommon to have snow on the mountains overlooking valleys and plains where fruit trees are in full bloom. Winters are biting cold while summers offer scorching heat. Torrential rainstorms and massive flooding can be easily followed by years of drought.

- St. Paul's first missionary tour took him to (modern day) Bosnia and Croatia.

- Many believe Jericho to be the world's oldest true city, dating its inhabitants all the way back to about 9000 B.C. It was sacked by the Israelites under Joshua's leadership (and with Rahab's help - remember *T3?*). Jericho is also the site of Jesus' visit with Zacchaeus.

- Mary, Martha and their brother Lazarus lived in Bethany, only about two miles from Jerusalem and very close to Jesus' birthplace (Bethlehem).

NOTES

Listen to the King

'Cause Jesus says so...

There are countless simple truths in Gospels, truths that many sort of "take for granted" as they grow older. It astounds me the number of Christians today (Catholics included) who disagree with fundamental Scriptural beliefs. Sometimes it's a matter of people taking the Bible out of context, sure. There are other times, though, that people fundamentally disagree with truths that come straight out of Jesus' mouth.

There's a problem if any "Christian" disagrees with Christ, isn't there?

The gospel reminds that Christ's voice is the source of truth:

"(Jesus said) ... for this I have come into the world, to bear witness to the truth. Every one who is of the truth hears my voice." **–John 18:37**

Put simply, if we only believe those Scriptural passages that we agree with than it's not really the Bible we believe in, is it?

So, here are a few things that **Jesus**, Himself, tells us in the Gospel. It's not a complete list. It's not a perfect list. This is my list: a little "Top Ten" for myself and for you, my brothers and sisters (God's children).

Consider this your "crib sheet" to your own personal "vacation bible school":

God, the Creator of all, is your Father, your Daddy (see Mark 14:36).
He's not just a creator. He's not an ambivalent observer. He's not a caretaker. He's your Daddy. You can trust Him. You can believe in Him. Believing in God isn't foolish. Believing that you are the center of the universe ... that's foolish.

The devil is real (see Mark 1:13; Luke 10:18).
He is not a myth or a figment of your imagination. He does exist and he doesn't want you anywhere near God. Resist him (James 4:8-9). And if you don't believe he's real, he's already won. The greatest thing the devil ever accomplished was making people believe that he doesn't exist.

Sin destroys you and will kill you (see Matthew 5:30; Mark 9:42).
It doesn't "just make you feel bad." It isn't something you can rationalize away. Sin destroys your capacity to love rightly and to live well. Sin also destroys your capacity to receive love. This is a serious thing. If you are in sin, reconcile yourself to God.

Not everyone is getting into heaven. (see Matthew 7:13-14).
It's a popular misconception that "all roads lead to heaven." That's just not true. Not everyone is getting into heaven, in fact many who think they are, probably aren't according to Scripture. Heaven is a decision, a gift from God chosen by the life you live. Hell is a choice, too. God wants you in Heaven.

God's mercy is bigger than your sins (see John 8:11; Luke 10:37).
The only sin God won't forgive is the sin you won't ask forgiveness for ... His mercy is limitless, but you have to be open to it. (Guilt doesn't come from God, it comes from within us. Your conscience is one of God's greatest gifts to you ... it's a gift, not a curse).

If you want to see God, look at Jesus (see John 14:9).
Jesus wasn't just a philosopher or a prophet. He is God. No other religious leader of consequence ever claimed to actually "be" God. No lunatic would live what He lived. No other leader rose from the dead. No other leader is coming back again. If you're trying to figure out what God wants, get to know Jesus.

If you want to know Jesus, ask the Holy Spirit to guide you (see John 16:7, 13).
The same way Jesus reveals the Father, the Holy Spirit reveals Christ. Ask the Holy Spirit to lead you closer to Jesus. Ask him to show you Christ's face, help you to hear His voice and give you the courage to follow Jesus' will.

Leader's Note

Many people quote the Bible and do not know who they are actually quoting. In the "Listen to the King" section, there are ten very easy-to-remember but very often forgotten truths that Christ Himself gives us. These truths, if pondered regularly and prayed upon daily, have the ability to transform not only your teenagers' lives but your own as well.

On a side note, if you as a leader share the simplest truths of the Gospel without taking them to heart personally, or if you proclaim them without letting them change your daily life, the teens will recognize your hypocrisy. Teenagers can smell a fake–and they usually point it out in a direct and unashamed manner.

In this section, make time to read through each truth and continually remind your young people that these words came from Christ Himself. While all the words of Scripture are inspired by God and all Scripture is absolutely sacred, the gospels hold a special place in the Bible. May we never forget this truth and may our lives proclaim that we believe it.

Listen to the King

God will give you what you need (see Matthew 7:7-12).
He might not always give you what you want, but God will always give you what you need. That difference seems small but it's huge; it seems easy, but living it is difficult. It takes trust.

In your life you'll have troubles; that doesn't mean God doesn't love you (see John 16:33).
"Bad times" don't mean that God doesn't care. Jesus never promised that once you follow God you'd never struggle again. He promised that God won't abandon you.

The Eucharist is Christ's true flesh and blood
(see Matthew 26:26; John 6:22-58).
It's not a symbol. It's not a simple memorial. It's more than that. The Eucharist is how Christ insures that He is with us forever (Matthew 28:20). The apostles didn't misunderstand. The Church didn't "make it up". St. Paul believed in the real presence, too (1 Corinthians 11:23-29).

Oh, and just two more truths, for the road:

The Bible is not outdated, it is timeless; it is the Living Word of God.

Jesus loves you, this I know...

Notes

FINDING "THE KINGDOM" IN MATTHEW

The King and His Kingdom are referenced about six-dozen times in the gospel of Matthew. Wondering why we called this study *Thy Kingdom Come*? Well, wonder no more.

Take some time to read and pray through these verses, and you will soon see that Christ's words were far more than "symbolic." As the study points out, Christ is the fulfillment of the Kingdom, and that Kingdom is God's Church on earth.

But don't take our word for it, explore His ...

Verses from Matthew that point back to the King and His Kingdom:

1:6
2:1-3
2:9
3:2
4:17, 23
5:3, 10, 19-20, 35
6:10, 33
7:21
8:11-12
9:35
10:7
11:11-12
12:25-26, 28
13:11, 19, 24, 31-33, 38, 41-47, 52
14:9
16:19, 28
18:1-4, 23
19:12-14, 23-24
20:1, 21
21:5, 31, 43
22:2, 7, 11, 13
24:7, 14
25:1, 34, 40
26:29
27:11, 29, 37, 42

LEADER'S NOTE

No gospel discusses the Kingdom as much as the gospel of Matthew. You can say share that fact with your young people but until you actually see how many places and times Matthew refers to this "Kingdom" it might not seem very important. This is one of those areas your credibility can be bolstered as a leader; it is one thing for a leader to say that the key theme is the kingdom of God, but it is another to say it and then systematically prove the fact. By doing so you are not only proving this truth but you are showing sharing insight into the authorship and purpose of St. Matthew's work.

The more secure they feel in the gospel of St. Matthew and have those themes reinforced, the more open they will be to the other gospels, to learning about them and sharing them.

NOTES

NOTES

NOTES

NOTES

ADDITIONAL RESOURCES

The Great Adventure: A Journey through the Bible by Jeff Cavins

The Theology of the Body by Pope John Paul II

The Theology of the Body Explained by Christopher West

The Theology of the Body for Teens by Jason & Crystalina Evert and Brian Butler

To Know Christ by Frank Sheed

Theology and Sanity by Frank Sheed

You Can Understand the Bible by Peter Kreeft

A Father Who Keeps His Promises by Scott Hahn

Thayer's Lexicon with Strong's Exhaustive Concordance

Ask the Bible Geek®: Answers to Questions from Catholic Teens by Mark Hart

Blessed are the Bored in Spirit: A Young Catholic's Search for Meaning by Mark Hart

Ask the Bible Geek® 2: It's About Time by Mark Hart

Hahn, Scott. "Understanding the Scriptures. A Complete Course on Bible Study." Midwest Theological Forum.